TOMBOY

Queer Film Classics

Edited by Matthew Hays and Thomas Waugh

The enduring commercial success of LGBTQ2I films over recent generations offers proof of widespread interest in queer film within both pop culture and academia. Not only are recent works riding the wave of the new maturity of queer film culture, but a century of queer and proto-queer classics are in busy circulation thanks to a burgeoning online queer cinephile culture and have been brought back to life by omnipresent festivals and revivals. Meditations on individual films from queer perspectives are particularly urgent, unlocking new understandings of political as well as aesthetic and personal concerns.

Queer Film Classics at McGill-Queen's University Press emphasizes good writing, rigorous but accessible scholarship, and personal, reflective thinking about the significance of each film – writing that is true to the film, original, and enlightening and enjoyable for film buffs, scholars, and students alike. Books in the series are short – roughly 40,000 words – but well illustrated and allow for considerable depth. Exploring historical, authorial, and production contexts and drawing on filmic analysis, these open-ended essays also develop the author's personal interests or a subjective reading of the work's sexual identity discourses or reception. The series aims to meet the diversity, quality, and originality of classics in the queer film canon, broadly conceived, with equally compelling writing and critical insight. Books in the series have much to teach us, not only about the art of film but about the queer ways in which films can transmit our meanings, our stories, and our dreams.

L'Homme blessé
Robert Payne

Boys Don't Cry
Chase Joynt and Morgan M Page

Orlando
Russell Sheaffer

Appropriate Behavior
Maria San Filippo

Midnight Cowboy
Jon Towlson

À tout prendre et *Il était une fois dans l'Est*
Julie Vaillancourt

Anders als die Andern
Ervin Malakaj

Maurice
David Greven

Winter Kept Us Warm
Chris Dupuis

The Children's Hour
Julia Erhart

Y Tu Mamá También
Juan Llamas-Rodriguez

Tomboy
Cristina Johnston

TOMBOY

Cristina Johnston

McGill-Queen's University Press
Montreal & Kingston | London | Chicago

ISBN 978-0-2280-2375-3 (cloth)
ISBN 978-0-2280-2376-0 (paper)
ISBN 978-0-2280-2528-3 (ePDF)
ISBN 978-0-2280-2529-0 (ePUB)

Legal deposit second quarter 2025
Bibliothèque et Archives nationales du Québec

Printed in Canada on acid-free paper that is 100% ancient-forest-free, containing 100% sustainable, recycled fibre, and processed chlorine-free.

McGill-Queen's University Press in Montreal is on land which long served as a site of meeting and exchange amongst Indigenous Peoples, including the Haudenosaunee and Anishinabeg nations. In Kingston it is situated on the territory of the Haudenosaunee and Anishinaabek. We acknowledge and thank the diverse Indigenous Peoples whose footsteps have marked these territories on which peoples of the world now gather.

Library and Archives Canada Cataloguing in Publication

Title: Tomboy / Cristina Johnston.
Names: Johnston, Cristina, author
Series: Queer film classics (McGill-Queen's University Press)
Description: Series statement: Queer film classics | Includes bibliographical references and index.
Identifiers: Canadiana (print) 20250134799 | Canadiana (ebook) 20250134829 | ISBN 9780228023760 (paper) | ISBN 9780228023753 (cloth) | ISBN 9780228025283 (ePDF) | ISBN 9780228025290 (ePUB)
Subjects: LCSH: Sciamma, Céline, 1980-—Criticism and interpretation. | LCSH: Tomboy (Motion picture) | LCSH: Tomboys in motion pictures. | LCSH: Coming-of-age films—France—History and criticism.
Classification: LCC PN1997.2.T654 J64 2025 | DDC 791.43/72—dc23

This book was designed and typeset by studio oneonone in Minion 11/14.
Copyediting by Kathryn Simpson.

McGill-Queen's University Press
Suite 1720, 1010 Sherbrooke St West, Montreal, QC, H3A 2R7

Authorized safety representative in the EU: Mare Nostrum Group BV, Mauritskade 21D, 1091 GC Amsterdam, the Netherlands, gpsr@mare-nostrum.co.uk

In memory of Kat Lindner

Contents

Acknowledgments

First and foremost, my thanks go to Tom Waugh and Matt Hays for their endless patience, for the generosity and good humour of their feedback at all stages of this project, and for having agreed to include *Tomboy* and Céline Sciamma as part of the new group of Queer Film Classics in the first place. Thanks, too, to the three anonymous reviewers for their careful reading of the manuscript and their unerringly helpful, generous, and insightful comments, to everyone at McGill-Queen's University Press for their advice, guidance, and support, and in particular to Jonathan Crago for his much-appreciated, never-faltering cheerleading over the past few years.

My friends and colleagues at the University of Stirling have put up with me whittering on about Sciamma for quite some time, and for that I am extremely grateful. Particular thanks to Fiona Barclay, Susan Berridge, Jean-Michel DesJacques, Christine Ferguson, Hannah Grayson, Aedín ní Loingsigh, and Nina Parish for their willingness to listen with great kindness to some of the ideas that have made their way into this book, and for their thoughtful questions and suggestions. I am especially grateful to Ali Cathcart, whose friendship, excellent company, and encouragement over the final months of revisions were invaluable. Thanks to Brigitte Depret and Mathilde Mazau for their helpful advice on linguistic points, to Bill Marshall for his insightful comments, to David Murphy for answering random queries with great patience and a healthy dose of sarcasm, and to Kirsty Alexander, Finn

Mackie, Mihaela Mihai, Michaëlle Petit, and Mathias Thaler for innumerable Sciamma-related conversations.

Work on this book began against the rather unusual backdrop of the Covid-19 pandemic and lockdowns, which brought with them an array of challenges, including a period of homeschool and much domestic juggling. The final stages of revisions were also written against a difficult backdrop and my gratitude and love go to Kerri, Lola, and Maya, without whom none of this would ever have been written. Thank you for having been endlessly patient with me, for always buying the right biscuits, and for just generally making everything better all the time.

This book is dedicated to Kat Lindner, with whom I had the great pleasure of working on Sciamma for the first time and without whom, among many other things, I would still be distractedly referring to *Cécile* Sciamma. Kat was a great colleague and friend, and I will always be very proud and grateful to have known her.

Synopsis

A young child sits on what seems to be their father's knee in the driving seat of a car; the car makes its way through the quiet streets of an anonymous French suburban backdrop. Under the father's instruction the child is driving the car, spindly arms stretched out gripping the steering wheel, giggling as they try to understand in which direction to flick the indicator for a right turn. We then watch father and child carry boxes through a small housing estate and we meet two other family members – a younger child, and the children's heavily pregnant mother. All four of them are settling into their new home.

Our would-be driver watches a group of children playing on the grass below the family's apartment and wanders down. By the time they arrive, most of the children have gone but a young girl watches on, asking "t'es le nouveau?" (Are you the new boy?) After a brief hesitation the new child nods, and the girl introduces herself as Lisa. There is no reciprocal mutual introduction, so she asks:

"Don't you want to tell me your name?"

"Mikaël. My name is Mikaël."

The pair then go off to find the other children who are playing in the forest. Lisa introduces Mikaël and convinces the others to allow them to join in with their game. It is only back in the apartment a little later that we discover that as far as their family is concerned, this child is not Mikaël but Laure – that is, a girl, not a boy.

As the film unfolds, Mikaël/Laure becomes part of the group of children enjoying their summer holidays outdoors. As a group the children play football, have water fights, and go swimming in the local lake. A closer friendship develops between Lisa and Mikaël/Laure, and then gently edges towards a romantic relationship. They walk together in the forest, hold hands, and kiss. They also dance together in Lisa's bedroom and Lisa applies makeup to Mikaël/Laure's face to see what they look like "as a girl." Initially, the other family members are unaware that Laure is passing as Mikaël until Lisa comes to call on Mikaël while only Jeanne, the younger sister, is at home. Jeanne then uses the knowledge to her advantage, making Mikaël/Laure promise to allow her to come and play with the older children in exchange for not "revealing" that Mikaël is also Laure.

At one point all the children are out playing together and a child pushes Jeanne over; her knee is hurt and she is upset. Someone tells Mikaël/Laure what has happened and they fight with the other child, pinning him to the ground and hitting him. Back home, as Mikaël/Laure patches up Jeanne's scratches, the doorbell rings. At the door are Rayan, Mikaël/Laure's opponent from the fight, and his mother, looking for an explanation and an apology from "Mikaël." Mikaël/Laure's mother is confused but says that she will "have words" with her child, and then closes the door. A tense evening follows: the mother's anger, surprise, and incomprehension boil over and she slaps Mikaël/Laure before sending them to their room. A little later, Mikaël/Laure's father comes to find them, explaining that they should not be angry with their mother. But the father does not ask Mikaël/Laure to explain what has been happening. Later still, Jeanne arrives and climbs into bed with her sibling, too young to explicitly express her concern but clearly shaken by the events of the evening and keen to be with Mikaël/Laure.

The following morning, the mother comes to wake Mikaël/Laure up, first asking a sleepy Jeanne to go back to her own bed. As Mikaël/Laure pulls on their customary pair of shorts, the mother forcefully insists on a blue dress instead, in an act of "deliberate humiliation" (Handyside 2023, 164). The mother takes Mikaël/Laure first to Rayan's home and then to see Lisa, to explain that they are Laure. The mother's explanations occur offscreen while the camera remains focused on Mikaël/Laure, who stands quietly in another room. Lisa is out when they go to her house, so Mikaël/Laure's mother asks if they can wait for her. When Lisa returns and finds out – again off camera, out of our earshot – that Mikaël is Laure, she comes to find her friend. There is a silent exchange of glances between the two children before Lisa walks away. Mikaël/Laure runs out of the apartment and keeps running until they reach the forest, where they sit alone and visibly distressed.

As Mikaël/Laure walks through the woods, having left the blue dress limply hanging in the branches of a tree and dressed once again in shorts and a T-shirt, they come across the other children and initially observe them through the trees. The inevitable happens: a branch cracks, Mikaël/Laure's presence is discovered, and the other children chase them. Finally the children catch up with Mikaël/Laure and corner them against a tree. In a profoundly disturbing scene, the children then insist on "checking" Mikaël/Laure's biological sex by getting them to unzip their shorts. Lisa intervenes but, rather than managing to stop the children, instead they force her to be the one who "checks." As viewers, we only hear the sound of the zipper, and the scene ends with Mikaël/Laure alone again, sitting at the foot of the tree.

We cut to the day before the new school year is due to begin, and to Mikaël/Laure, Jeanne, and their father gathered around the mother on the bed with a very young newborn on her belly. The mother suggests that Mikaël/Laure might want to go out and enjoy the last day of the holidays but Mikaël/Laure says no and wanders to the kitchen, grabs a snack from the cupboard, and drifts out to the balcony to gaze down at the world below. Downstairs, gazing up at the balcony, is Lisa. Another cut and we are outside with the two children facing each other as they had done in their initial encounter. Lisa speaks first: "What's your name?" A moment of silence follows, then "My name is Laure." A smile begins to take shape on Mikaël/Laure's face and the screen goes black. The credits roll to the joyous sound of Para One's theme tune.

Credits

Tomboy, 2011, France, French, 82 min
Colour, Sound, 35mm, 1.85: 1
Shot in Torcy and Vaires (Seine-et-Marne, France)
Distributed in France by Pyramide Distribution, in the US by Dada Films (theatrical), Rocket Releasing (theatrical and subtitled), the Criterion Channel (TV and digital), and Wolfe Video (DVD), and in the UK by Peccadillo Pictures (theatrical) and BBC Four and BBC Two (TV)
Production companies: Hold Up Films, Arte France Cinéma (co-production), Lilies Film (co-production), Canal+ and ARTE (participation), La Région Île-de-France (support), in partnership with the Centre National du Cinéma et de l'Image Animée (CNC) and in association with Arte/Cofinova 6 and Playtime
Director: Céline Sciamma
Writer: Céline Sciamma
Producers: Bénédicte Couvreur, Rémi Burah (co-producer), and Tiphaine Perin (assistant producer)

Premiere: 10 February 2011 at Berlin International Film Festival, and in France on 20 April 2011.
For festivals, prizes, and nominations, see the introduction.

Principal Cast
Mikaël/Laure: Zoé Héran
Jeanne: Malonn Lévana
Lisa: Jeanne Disson
Mikaël/Laure's mother: Sophie Cattani
Mikaël/Laure's father: Mathieu Demy
Rayan: Rayan Boubekri
Vince: Yohan Vero
Noah: Noah Vero
Cheyenne: Cheyenne Lainé
Lisa's mother: Christel Baras
Rayan's mother: Valérie Roucher

Crew
Cinematography: Crystel Fournier
Film editing: Julien Lacheray
Production design: Thomas Grézaud
Music by: Jean-Baptiste de Laubier (as Para One) and Jérôme Echenoz (co-composer)
Sound editing: Sébastien Savine
Casting: Christel Baras

TOMBOY

Chapter 1

Introduction: Childhood, Gender, and Queer Selfhood

Released in 2011, Céline Sciamma's *Tomboy* is the central work in her "coming-of-age" trilogy, nestled between *Naissance des pieuvres* (*Water Lilies*, 2007) and *Bande de filles* (*Girlhood*, 2014). All three films share a similarly tightly defined focus: *Water Lilies* examines girlhood and teenage desire; *Girlhood*'s focus is on the lives of a group of Black girls in their late teens living in the suburbs of Paris, while *Tomboy* offers a quiet exploration of the experiences and burgeoning friendships of a ten-year-old child who moves to a new town during the summer holidays, first introducing themselves to others as Mikaël.

It is only some six minutes later that we learn that, for their parents and younger sister, Mikaël is "Laure," the "figure of the gender nonconformist child [representing] a relatively recent addition to the identities portrayed within visual culture" (Waldron 2013, 60). The film creatively uses the shifting sands of late childhood and early adolescence to suggest neither a straightforward passage from one stage to the other, nor an uncomplicated depiction of "passing" as "one or the other" in binary gendered terms or in terms of any single fixed category, whether lesbian, trans, trans*, or butch, for example. Rather, Sciamma's approach offers space for a kind of "fractal" thinking about gender (Halberstam 2002, 366); *Tomboy* is an understated examination of childhood, gender, and queer selfhood. Sciamma also determinedly avoids a psychologizing unpacking of Mikaël/Laure's behaviour, actions, or motivations. In "a gesture of refusal (of cinematic conventions and societal expectations)" (Lindner 2018, 204), Sciamma does not seek to analyze *why* Laure

Figure 1
"Mikaël. My name is Mikaël."

wants to pass as Mikaël but rather to think about *how* this occurs, and how Mikaël/Laure acts and responds to situations. With this aim, through what has, since *Tomboy*'s release, become her characteristic engagement with the surfaces, textures, fluids, and materials of individual lived experience, in this case those of late childhood (tree bark, flesh, urine, Play-Doh, spaghetti), Sciamma allows queer potentialities to unfold subtly, without working towards a neatly disentangled vision of what lies beyond the summer.

Tomboy premiered at the Berlinale on 10 February 2011 as the opening film in the Panorama section and went on to win the Teddy Jury Award, which is awarded annually at Berlin to LGBTQI+-themed films. Following success there, the film, its cast, and its crew amassed an array of prizes, from Best Actress at the Buenos Aires International Film Festival for Zoé Héran's performance in the lead role to the Golden Duke Grand Prix Award for Céline Sciamma at the Odessa Film Festival. *Tomboy* also garnered multiple further nominations in France and beyond.[1] This is really not bad going, considering that the film was written in the space of a month, cast over a three-week period (Dokhan 2011), and then shot over twenty days with a crew of fourteen. Moreover the cast was mostly children (only four adults appear onscreen: Mikaël/Laure's mother and father and the mothers of two of their friends, all of whom are nameless characters), and the movie had a limited budget (Frois 2011). And to top it all off, *Tomboy* was only writer/director Céline Sciamma's second full-length production.

Tomboy was released in France a couple of months after its initial screening in Berlin, on 20 April 2011, to almost exclusively positive acclaim. Critics heaped praise on the film for its "extreme sensitivity" (Frois 2011),[2] for its ability to "avoid all the traps of films about childhood" (de Bruyn 2011), for the "beauty" and "strength" of Sciamma's vision (Baurez 2011), and for its "tenderness" (Lefort 2011). That praise was largely repeated later the same year when the film was released on DVD in France, though some reviewers did grumpily note the dearth of bonus material on the DVD (Libiot 2011). The only extras are an interview with the director and a handful of trailers.

The narratives of Sciamma's triptych are largely recounted from the perspective of girls and young women and, in the case of *Tomboy*, from the perspective of a "gender nonconformist child" (Waldron 2013, 60). The three films do not form a trilogy in the strict sense. They do not revisit the same cast of characters, nor indeed the same geographical setting, nor do they offer different episodes of a singular story. Rather, their status as a trilogy stems from the exploration of perspectives often marginalized in French cinema and from an explicit desire to examine key stages of the development of their child and teenage protagonists with clear political, sexual, and aesthetic parallels across all three films, emphasizing "the need for agency of children and adolescents, binding this imperative into [Sciamma's] aesthetic choices and modes of filmmaking" (Wilson 2021, 2).

Naissance des pieuvres centres on three characters in their mid-teens: Marie (Pauline Acquart), Anne (Louise Blachère), and Floriane (Adèle Haenel). Floriane is the star of the local synchronized swimming team, and captures Marie's gaze during a competition. The film depicts the complexities of teenage friendships, love, and sexual attraction, as Marie falls for the apparently supremely confident Floriane and Anne tries to attract the attention of François (Warren Jacquin) – a member of the water polo team who, to make matters more complicated, is also going out with Floriane. *Tomboy*, as we know, focuses on a younger cast of characters – ten-year-old Mikaël/Laure, their six-year-old sister Jeanne, and the group of friends they develop over the course of the summer holidays in an anonymous French suburb. *Bande de filles* also centres on a small group of characters, this time the "bande de filles" (girl gang) of the title, all young Black women in their late teens: Marième (who also comes to be known as Vic, and is played by Karidja Touré), Lady (Assa Silla), Adiatou (Lindsay Karamoh), and Fily (Mariétou Touré).

In this book I argue that *Tomboy* has opened up new avenues for cinematic representations of queer characters. I will discuss the film's depiction of gendered identities in that context, but I will also examine the language of contemporaneous reviews and general reception, as well as my own linguistic choices – most notably in relation to the use of gendered pronouns. These issues matter and, while I hope they do not get in the way of a reading of the book, I am conscious of the importance of acknowledging the choices I am making. Sciamma does not explicitly steer the film into a discussion of trans childhood and I am also not keen to impose my own terms and definitions on the film and its preoccupations, as far as possible, to avoid limiting the possibilities that Mikaël/Laure's experiences might otherwise open up to audiences. In this context, it is perhaps helpful to bear in mind Jack Halberstam's use of the term "trans*," precisely to "emphasise the bagginess of the category of transgender, and to refuse the conventional work of easy classification that such terminology usually performs" (2022, 187). In my own linguistic usage, I have opted for the pronouns "they" and "them" to refer to the central character, and I have also chosen to refer to the protagonist as "Mikaël/Laure" except in scenes where two presentations of self occur. For example, the child is called "Laure" by their mother even though we have heard them referring to themselves as "Mikaël."

My punctuation choice is also deliberate: I chose to use a slash (/) between Mikaël and Laure rather than, for instance, a hyphen. French-Algerian feminist scholar Hélène Cixous suggests that the hyphen has a heightened ability to "reflect the complexity of intersubjective relationships" (Kilduff 2018, 202). This child's subjectivity is complex and multi-layered, it is not a fixed thing, and I am very much interested in "the multitude of ties that weave and bind us together and the ever-changing unfixed nature of them" (Kilduff 2018, 202). Nevertheless, my concern is that the hyphen might bring the baggage of terms vying for priority; that it implies a tension to be negotiated; and, at least on my reading of *Tomboy*, that this is not what Mikaël/Laure is doing. Mikaël and Laure are, in large part, names we hear being used to refer to the same person in public versus domestic settings, respectively. As I will discuss more fully later, as the film progresses the porosity of the public and domestic spheres becomes ever more evident. I am wary of the tension that hyphenation might imply, and have thus opted for the use of the "/" in most instances. I hope that this use of the slash will help emphasize that there is one individual here, "a single entity made up of imitations and multiple identities superimposed throughout the film"[3] (Chevalier 2019, 72). The fact that Mikaël/Laure is one person makes it significant that the language used to describe their identity is different depending on the context; their singular identity and multiple names can also be *read* in different ways depending on the context.

To return to the trilogy, Sciamma's first three films are, above all, thematically linked by an interest in childhood and adolescence and in the ways in which marginalized experiences thereof might be depicted onscreen. Cinematically, Sciamma positions herself between French and American traditions in this regard, commenting, for example: "I like the sensitive look of traditional French films and the fact that the children are often portrayed as rebels, but I also like the way the American tradition stylises everything and is full of fantasy around childhood" (Pryor 2011). Asked, across numerous interviews, to cite her points of cinematic reference in the representation of childhood, François Truffaut's *Les 400 Coups* (*The 400 Blows*, 1959) and *L'Argent de poche* (*Small Change*, 1976) come up as regularly as *E.T.* (Spielberg, 1982), *Mysterious Skin* (Araki, 2004), or, most often in relation to *Bande de filles*, Richard Linklater's *Boyhood*, a point of reference that stems far more from the coincidence of the two films' release in the same year than from any genuine similarities or parallels in approach or from any deliberate strategy on Sciamma's part.[4] The coincidence did, nevertheless, offer a handy bit of wordplay for Anglophone headline writers.[5] The number of cinematic influences Sciamma was asked about over the course of the initial round of press coverage of *Tomboy* in spring 2011 was so noteworthy that Sciamma commented on it herself in a short interview in the weekly French magazine *Télérama* (Odicino 2011) on the occasion of the first screening of the film on French TV on Canal+ in July 2011: "It's true that if you draw together all the references critics pinned on me, you could think I've made a kind of *Boys Don't Cry*, but with Pialat's style, and set in the childhood America of 1980s Spielberg!"

Filming Childhood and Adolescence in French Cinema

The sustained interest across the "trilogy" in childhood and adolescence as the loci of specific anxieties, where identities are formed and troubled and challenged, also makes sense in terms of a lineage of cinematic representations of childhood. As others have noted, "childhood has a peculiar subjective status in most modern societies … [and] the figure of the child … oscillates between agency and allegory" (Hemelryk Donald, Wilson, and Wright 2018, 2). For Sciamma, those anxieties and identities particularly coalesce around questions of gender and sexualities. And while the director herself notes laconically that the dearth of films dealing with such questions in childhood and adolescence makes her both "a feminist and an opportunist" (Vallet 2012), as Katharina Lindner observes, Sciamma's films in fact open up new ground insofar as they "engage centrally with questions of gender and sexuality while refraining from inscribing rigid gender and sexual identities onto their characters" (2018, 194). In so doing they give rise to what we can understand as "queer resonances" (2018, 8), which are particularly uncommon in cinematic representations of childhood.

This is not to say that there are no other French films focusing on child or adolescent characters that have dealt with questions of gender, sexuality, and desire. After all, as Romain Chareyron and Gilles Viennot write in the introduction to their edited volume *Screening Youth: Contemporary French and Francophone Cinema*, the frequency with which the authors in their collection engage with "questions of gender and sexuality underscore[s] their primal significance in contemporary youth narratives" (2019, 8). For Gemma Edney in the same collection: "Youth has long been a central concern of French cinema" and recent years have seen "a major surge in films dealing with the youth experience, with an ever-growing number of filmmakers turning to youth as a main concern" (2019, 21). Indeed, I have already highlighted in these opening pages how frequently Sciamma was asked to comment upon the impact of cinematic touchstones like *The 400 Blows* or *Small Change* in interviews around *Tomboy*'s release. There are numerous other examples I could mention in French film history, from Jean Vigo's *Zéro de conduite* (*Zero for Conduct*, 1933) through to Claude Miller's *L'Effrontée* (*An Impudent Girl*, 1985) and more recent works such as *Mignonnes* (*Cuties*, 2020) by Maïmouna Doucouré or *Divines* directed by Uda Benyamina (2016), often with a core focus on the troubled masculinity of young boys or the troubling agency of young girls.

I nevertheless suggest that there is something atypical about *Tomboy* against this long-established backdrop. While Edney, Chareyron, and Viennot are absolutely correct to highlight the long history of these questions in "youth cinema," as their work also indicates, this focus tends to arise in films centred on characters in their adolescent years. As they are quite rightly quick to point out, their choice of "youth cinema" as the label under which to categorize the films analyzed in their collection is a product of the term's "semantic flexibility" that enables them to circumvent "the risk of creating artificial – and often counter-productive – boundaries between these different stages of life" (Chareyron and Viennot 2019, 2). And I am conscious that, insofar as Mikaël/Laure is ten years old and Héran was eleven during the shoot (twelve by the time it was released), we are certainly on the *cusp* of their teenage years but we are not there yet. We are watching *children* in *Tomboy* and exploring these same questions from the perspective of their lived experience, disentangling the "queer resonances" of the behaviours and actions of children.

I suggest that this is doubly important because the focus in "youth films" is often not solely or even necessarily predominantly on the young person (whether child or teenager) at the core of their narratives. Rather, they tend to be films that examine, for example, what happens when those individuals' gendered or sexual identities and their burgeoning desires are challenged by, or in some way come into conflict with, societal norms. And those norms are often given voice through the microcosm of a family structure or a social structure such as the school. As we will see later, the family setting is certainly important in *Tomboy*. However, in many ways it is inclusion within and exclusion from the peer group that is more central to the film's concerns. Whether in relation to Mikaël/Laure's gendered identity or in terms of their non-gender-specific experience as the new kid in town trying to make friends, at the heart of the film are the relationships between Mikaël/Laure and Lisa, their sister, and the other children. The focus remains almost exclusively on the actions of children, with grown-ups peripheral and occupying comparatively little screen time. This was unusual when *Tomboy* was released and I would argue that it remains atypical.

Narratives of Queer Childhood

There are, of course, rare but important examples that have trod similar ground in a representation of queer childhood or of queer narratives of selfhood in childhood over recent decades. Karine Espineira, whose work focuses primarily on depictions of "transidentités"[6] on French TV, rather than in the cinema, identifies a significant representational shift that has occurred since the 2000s, building on the "very fact that a portion of the cisgender audience is now familiar with questions of gender and with trans issues," though also underlining the fact that "if we consider the evolution of trans movements," the *range* of representations remains "limited" (2021).[7] However, the corpus in Espineira's study almost exclusively examines "transidentités" in adult characters.

Here I would like to consider two cinematic texts, namely Belgian director Alain Berliner's 1997 *Ma Vie en rose* (*My Life in Pink*) and the more recent *Petite Fille* (*Little Girl*) by Sébastien Lifschitz (2020). Both films tackle some of the same questions as *Tomboy* and, crucially, they are also centred on preteen characters.[8] However, while there are certainly parallels to be drawn between their central figures and the queer narratives of selfhood that they are navigating, they do so in very different ways – different both from *Tomboy* and, indeed, from each other.

Ma Vie en rose uses a bubble-gum colour scheme that we might associate with Tim Burton's vision of suburbia circa *Edward Scissorhands* (1990), alongside "whimsical dream sequences [that] play on Ludovic's escapist fantasies and naïve ignorance of society's heteronormative gender constraints" (English 2019, 34). While Berliner does present us with a central character, Ludo (Georges du Fresne), who explicitly wants to be a girl when he grows up, much more is made of the conflict between Ludo's presentation of self and his father's concerns and objections, as well as between Ludo and mainstream society, as represented via the neighbours in their candy-coloured suburb. Whereas *Tomboy* has only four adults characters, Ludo's story is framed by

Figure 2
Ludo in *Ma Vie en rose.*

adults, as evidenced by a quick glance at the cast list, which includes not only his parents Pierre and Hanna (played by Jean-Philippe Écoffey and Michèle Laroque), but also his grandmother Élisabeth (Hélène Vincent), a cluster of adult neighbours, a psychoanalyst, and a schoolteacher. In contrast with the anonymity of the adults in *Tomboy*, most of the adults around Ludo are named, and we understand their relationships with each other and to him. *Ma Vie en rose* depicts the relationship between Ludo and his grandmother as particularly important to him, since Ludo's grandmother is initially the one figure who seems comfortable with his expression of self.

Looking back at the coverage of *Ma Vie en rose* now, though, and comparing it to the coverage of *Tomboy*, I am struck by two key similarities. On the one hand, at least in some reviews, Berliner was praised for avoiding the psychol-

Figure 3
Petite Fille.

ogizing of Ludo, or as Marie-Claude Martin writing in the now defunct Swiss publication *Le Nouveau Journal* put it: "Alain Berliner's great idea is to have left to one side all psychological artillery: he isn't setting out a case study and he doesn't try to explain it" (1997). His approach is praised as being "tender, generous" (Bradfer 1997) and "modest, genuine" (Nappey 1997). On the other hand – and I will examine parallels in my discussion of press coverage of *Tomboy* a little later – we also find genuinely shocking and appalling linguistic usage in some reviews. In an otherwise very positive review, for example, Katia Berger describes Ludo as "a hermaphrodite" (1997) or as a character "closer to Peter Pan than to a 'budding pederast'" (un pédéraste en herbe).

In contrast to the glorious colour schemes of *Ma Vie en rose*, its musical interludes, and its combination of fantasy and family melodrama, *Petite Fille* is a documentary by French gay filmmaker Sébastien Lifschitz focusing on Sasha, who is eight years old and was assigned male at birth but identifies as a girl. Lifschitz certainly shares an intimacy of gaze with Sciamma and, perhaps unsurprisingly in a documentary that is ostensibly about the experiences of a young child, we find some of the same visual markers of childhood I will analyze later in *Tomboy*, including a focus on games and playing, as well as on scenes that show us Sasha experimenting with her appearance in a mirror. However, as well as falling under distinct genre categories, *Tomboy* and *Petite Fille* are also telling importantly different stories, most notably through the latter's inclusion of Sasha's parents as central figures within the film. Indeed it is Sasha's mother, in particular, who narrates, or at the very least *frames*, her child's experience.

Very early on in the film she recounts her recollection of Sasha having told her, aged four, "Quand je serai grand, je serai une fille" (when I grow up, I'll be a girl – the gender distinction is interesting here with "grand" in the masculine singular form but "une fille" a feminine noun). While Sciamma steers away from the psychologizing of queer experiences, *Petite Fille*'s opening sequences show the mother in conversation with a psychologist who asks her to think back to her pregnancy, to whether she had thoughts about wanting a boy or a girl, to how she felt when she found out she would have a boy, and so on, a narrative that "satisfies the cisgender audience's assumptions about a trans story: that trans lives should be full of difficulty and strife, not only for the individual but also (if not mostly) for their relatives" (Fabre 2022, 32). While, to an extent, *Petite Fille* does explore some of the same territory as *Tomboy*, much more is made here of "the family's tireless struggle against a hostile environment as well as their everyday lives" (Berlinale 2020). Also, Sasha – unlike Mikaël/Laure – is shown as *actively* choosing her gender presentation.[9]

I am not explicitly stating that that is *not* the case for Mikaël/Laure – that there is no potential desire to "be" another gender – but rather the question is never posed. This may well be part of Mikaël/Laure's considerations but these are not given voice within the narrative of the film. Clearly, we can take the film's title – its use of an English word, rather than a French one – as a means of drawing our attention to one possible identity, namely Mikaël/Laure as "tomboy."[10] And we certainly see, especially in the latter stages of the film, the anger and fear of the mother in her rejection of a presentation as "tomboy." However, beyond the title and the title sequence, neither the English word nor its French equivalent is used in the film and so, for me, to draw conclusions about Mikaël/Laure's motivations would take us into the realm of speculation and, perhaps more significantly, into a world of "why" that Sciamma actively eschews. As Jeri English notes, in relation to *Ma Vie en rose* and *Tomboy*, it is significant that we are not watching "adults questioning their long-established gender identities or adolescents undergoing unwanted physical transformations, but rather prepubescent children whose certainty about their true gender identity disrupts the worldview of the adults around them" (2019, 33). I argue that this disruption features far less onscreen in *Tomboy* than in Berliner's work over a decade earlier but I would certainly agree that all three of these films – *Tomboy*, *Ma Vie en rose*, and *Petite Fille* – encourage us to consider the "disorientation" caused by such "disruption" and to see such disruption as ultimately positive.

Looking for Mikaël

After a tale of mid-teen lesbian desire against the backdrop of synchronized swimming in *Naissance des pieuvres*, and before audiences will explore the experiences of Black young women in the suburbs of Paris in *Bande de filles*, we have the story of Mikaël/Laure, a "navigat[ion] through the growing pains of the uncharted gender identity of a pre-pubescent girl" (Zulueta 2012, 107). The film begins with the arrival of Mikaël/Laure (Zoé Héran) and their family in their new home. Then comes the initial encounter between Mikaël/Laure and Lisa (Jeanne Disson), another child of roughly the same age, who reads Mikaël/Laure as male within a few seconds of their meeting. That encounter occurs around nine minutes into the film with no reference to the gender of the blond child having been made prior to that point. Lisa's assumption is neither avowedly accepted nor challenged by the Mikaël/Laure but rather it means that, when Lisa asks the newcomer their name, a context has been set up in which a conventionally male first name makes sense and becomes possible (Mikaël).

In some ways, thinking about *Tomboy* as a film about childhood that plays out against "an uncompromisingly realistic backdrop" (English 2019, 34), it is difficult to imagine an alternative outcome to this scene. Lisa's gendering of the child she meets happens so quickly, so unquestioningly, that it is hard to imagine a newly arrived ten-year-old having the courage to correct this more confident, more talkative child who has the advantage of being on home territory. It is also important, of course, that this scene takes place away from the gaze of the adults in these children's lives so there is nobody there who will "correct" Lisa's assumption. Lisa, we learn, has been watching Mikaël/Laure as they observed the other children playing from their balcony and, in this way, we have a first example of the ways in which "Laure … affirms their identity as Mikaël through the scrutiny of the other children" (English 2019, 34). Through Lisa, Mikaël/Laure will be introduced to the group of kids who hang around together and become part of the wider friendship group.

It is Mikaël/Laure's younger sister, six-year-old Jeanne, who first learns that the person she knows as Laure is known as Mikaël by the other children, and the shared knowledge becomes a point of complicity between the siblings, something they know but their parents do not. Sciamma does not shy away from the coercion that underpins that complicity. From early in the film, Jeanne has been eager to accompany Mikaël/Laure when they go out to play with the other children, a request that is consistently refused on the basis that Jeanne is "too young" (or, sometimes, no justification is offered). However, around forty-five minutes into the film, Jeanne is home alone while her father, we presume, is at work and her mother and Mikaël/Laure have gone shopping. The doorbell rings. The little girl opens the door and comes face-to-face with Lisa, who asks if Mikaël is there. Jeanne hesitates momentarily before saying that she is all alone at home. Lisa asks if she is Jeanne, which prompts the younger child's surprise as she asks, "Who are you?" Lisa seems equally taken aback by the question and introduces herself, asking, in a tone of mild bemusement, "Has he not mentioned me?" Jeanne tells her that he has but adds nothing more and Lisa leaves after a rather stilted "salut." Jeanne closes the door. The exchange is filmed as a classic shot–reverse shot sequence, flitting from Lisa to Jeanne and back again; the camera cuts to Jeanne, leaning against the inside of the closed front door, and to a close-up of her bemused expression.

When Mikaël/Laure and the mother return, laden with shopping bags, Jeanne is still sitting in the apartment's hallway. Mikaël/Laure walks past without noticing her but the mother spots her and asks, not seeming particularly concerned, what she is doing in the hall, suggesting she ended up there because she got bored waiting. Jeanne stands up and when Mikaël/Laure reappears in the hall, she says: "Lisa came looking for you." Mikaël/Laure stops in their tracks. After a brief pause, Jeanne continues: "She was looking for Mikaël." Jeanne lowers her voice to convey this information, clearly an indication that she knows this is something not to be communicated to their mother. Jeanne asks Mikaël/Laure why they are doing this, to which the latter responds that they are not doing anything. Jeanne clarifies: "You're pretending to be a boy." This is the only point in the film when Mikaël/Laure treats their younger sibling in an explicitly unkind and, indeed, threatening fashion, telling her to "shut up." They offer Jeanne no explanation for their actions. When Jeanne threatens to tell their mother, Mikaël/Laure pins the much smaller Jeanne to the wall. With their hand clamped over Jeanne's mouth, Mikaël/Laure initially orders her not to tell; then, still with their hand over her mouth, Mikaël/Laure promises to take Jeanne out to play every time for the rest of the summer. This is enough to placate the younger child.

The framing of these sequences is significant in its contribution to the depiction of an evident power imbalance between the two. Thus far, when filmed together, the two children have fit comfortably within the confines of the

Figure 4
Mikaël/Laure keeps Jeanne quiet.

frame, whether sitting at a table, or lying and playing on Jeanne's bed, or taking their bath together. This has also been true during play-fighting scenes early in the film. The visual emphasis is firmly placed on an equilibrium between the siblings despite the age difference. Here, however, we are suddenly reminded that Mikaël/Laure is older, bigger, and stronger than their younger sister. First, since part of the exchange is filmed with both children framed standing up, Mikaël/Laure seems to tower menacingly over Jeanne. Second, as the scuffle breaks out, the camera closes in and frames Jeanne in mid-close-up with only Mikaël/Laure's torso fitting the frame – another reminder of their physical difference. We watch as Jeanne squirms to try and move out from her sibling's grip, and we see Mikaël/Laure's hand firmly clamped across her mouth, as they manoeuvre their upper body to stop Jeanne from escaping or crying out.

From these coerced beginnings, the shared knowledge also triggers a second shift in the power balance between Mikaël/Laure and Jeanne in the sense that the former now has to allow Jeanne to come along to play with the other children. The first time we see them go out to play together with the larger group and then again later the same day when the family have dinner together, we see the ways in which Jeanne is trying to make sense of what is happening, building on her initial sense of surprise when Lisa came to the door. What I find particularly interesting is the fact that, from what Jeanne says, it is clear that she has an idea of what having a *brother* might mean and that it means something quite distinct from having a sister. While out with the other children, she meets Cheyenne (Cheyenne Lainé), who seems to be roughly the same age, and we observe them chatting about themselves, getting to know each other. Cheyenne explains that she has a sister and, in response, Jeanne talks about how great it is to have a big brother because a brother can "protect you and look after you." She even tells an imagined tale[11] that once, in their previous home, her "brother" stood up for her in front of the other kids, who never messed with her again because they were so scared of "him."

That evening, the family are eating dinner together. Jeanne and Mikaël/Laure are seated opposite each other and are quieter than usual, something their mother remarks upon. She asks Jeanne how things went that day and Jeanne explains that the friends are all nice but that her favourite was "Mikaël" because "he" played with her and carried her on his back. The two children exchange glances and burst out laughing, much to the confusion of their parents. What I find intriguing in these scenes is that Jeanne's words and her descriptions of "Mikaël," whether to Cheyenne or to her parents, tap into such clearly established gendered conventions: the older brother as protector and saviour, the new and slightly older male friend who has the physical strength to carry Jeanne.

Jeanne's imagined scenario of the protective older brother becomes a reality when Jeanne and Mikaël/Laure once again go out to play with the rest of the children and another child (Rayan – Rayan Boukekri) pushes Jeanne. We do not see the incident itself but only hear about it from Jeanne and another child, and we then see Mikaël/Laure getting into a fight with Rayan to defend their sister. This, in turn, triggers a visit from the other child and his mother later that day when they come to the family's apartment looking for "Mikaël," which clearly echoes the earlier scene when Lisa came to call on "Mikaël." However, the consequences on this occasion are more extreme because it is not a six-year-old child answering the door but rather Mikaël/Laure and Jeanne's mother, who comes face-to-face with Rayan and his mother.

The conversation between the two women begins offscreen as we watch Mikaël/Laure patching up Jeanne's grazed knee in another room. We hear the doorbell and see Mikaël/Laure's worried expression in close-up as their head quickly turns in the direction of the door, asking Jeanne what she thinks it might be. Muffled voices can be heard but we cannot make out what they are saying until the two children quietly walk through to the hall to join their mother. Jeanne stands next to her, but Mikaël/Laure hangs back a little and we hear Rayan's mother explaining: "'He says he got into a fight in the woods." Mikaël/Laure's mother looks rather blank, replying that she does not really see what that has to do with them, and Rayan's mother states: "He says it was your son." The children's mother continues to suggest that there must be some mistake, but then Rayan spots "Mikaël" and pipes up: "Yes, it was him. Mikaël." The latter's mother turns to gawp at her child, who stands silently for a few seconds before confirming: "Yes, it's true. It was me." The French wording is even more ambiguous than the English translation suggests because it could equally easily be understood as Mikaël/Laure confirming that they *are* the "Mikaël" to whom the other child refers. What is similar between the earlier scene with Lisa and this encounter with Rayan and his mother is that neither Jeanne nor Mikaël/Laure's mother gives Mikaël/Laure away. Both sister and mother respond to the external figure in a sufficiently ambiguous way to answer the outsiders' questions without "revealing" that Mikaël is also Laure. In both cases, it is through a direct exchange with Mikaël/Laure *after* the door has closed again on the outside world that the tensions bubble over and that Jeanne (in the earlier scene) and now Mikaël/Laure's mother give voice to their own confusion and incomprehension.

Before that exchange unfolds, though, and once the mother begins to realize what must have happened, she apologizes to Rayan's mother and reassures her that she will do "what's right." She is visibly shocked by the knowledge she is acquiring, and the force and clarity of her earlier statements become slightly less distinct as she adds, "Je vais l'punir." The elision between the pronoun (l') and the verb (punir) is hugely significant here because it is in the pronoun that the gender of the referent lies. Because the mother does not pronounce it clearly, we cannot be sure whether she is saying "je vais *le* punir" (I'll punish *him*) or "je vais *la* punir" (I'll punish *her*). Linguistically, there is nothing out of the ordinary about this indistinct usage. Truncation of certain words and types or words, elision between individual terms, is a perfectly standard element of spoken French. However, it is unusual in coming from the mother, first because thus far her speech has been extremely clearly enunciated, and second because it only occurs here on the one term that would ordinarily be unambiguously gendered. It is difficult not to read it as an attempt not to acknowledge the complexity of the situation she is facing, at least while there is a public audience to contend with.

To return to the scene, the mother instructs Mikaël/Laure to apologize and, once the door closes, she turns to face her child, a mixture of anger, shock, and incomprehension in her expression as tears begin to form. As striking as the string of questions she fires out is the fact that she uses her child's (domestic) name: "What have you done, Laure? What have you done? Why have you done this?" The child simply responds "I don't know," which prompts the mother to grab Mikaël/Laure by the arm – we don't see this gesture directly but the child jerks forward in a way that makes the action clear. More questions follow: "You told everyone you're a boy? You lied? And you dragged your sister into all this? Why did you do it? Eh?" Mikaël/Laure's lack of response is met with a sharp slap across the face, a moment of violence that obviously stuns the mother as much as the child. The former looks away, then down at the ground, eyes filled with tears, before ordering Mikaël/Laure to go to their room.

We then cut to a shot of Mikaël/Laure sitting on their bed, crying quietly, seemingly alone. As the camera tracks backwards, we realize that actually their father is next to them on the bed, silent and gazing down towards the floor. Given their obvious complicity in multiple earlier scenes, such as the tandem driving sequence, the fact that father and child do not look at each other serves to underscore the emotional violence left in the wake of physical violence. If we think back to English's observation that it is the "scrutiny of the other children" that enables Laure to be Mikaël, the inability of the parents to hold their child's gaze in these scenes – or even just to look at them – is doubly poignant.

The father speaks first, telling Mikaël/Laure not to be angry with their mother. The child offers no response. As the camera continues to track backwards, we see the father awkwardly putting his arm around his child's shoulders, offering unconvincing platitudes: "Don't worry. It'll be OK. Everything will turn out OK. It's already all done." Mikaël/Laure's only words underline the poignancy of the exchange: "Please can we leave this place." This time, it is the father who has no adequate response; his gaze simply falls to the ground once again.

There is then a final cut, this time to Mikaël/Laure lying awake in bed the same evening, no longer crying but now staring at the ceiling. We hear a door opening and Mikaël/Laure's momentarily concerned glance is quickly replaced by a smile as Jeanne wordlessly enters the room and climbs up in bed with her sibling. The camera remains fixed on the children's faces as they lie next to each other, not speaking, looking up at the ceiling together.[12] The silence is broken by what initially sounds like something of a non sequitur from Jeanne, who says: "I've got one for you." I will discuss this in more detail a little later, but here, I would just note two things. First, while we, as viewers, may be unsure precisely *what* she might have "one" of for Mikaël/Laure, the closeness between siblings is evident in Mikaël/Laure's instant comprehension that they are now switching into "game mode."

Second, the closeness between the pair is underlined further by the lengths of the silences that are allowed to play out between them. From when Jeanne

Figure 5
Mikaël/Laure and their father.

climbs into the bed until she says, "I've got one for you," a full twenty seconds elapse. That may not seem long in the grand scheme of things but, coming after the awkwardness – both physical and verbal – in the semi-silent encounter between father and child in the previous scene, we are struck by the ease with which the children are able to be in each other's silent company, and ultimately break the silence.

The following day, Mikaël/Laure's mother forces them to don a blue dress and takes them to first to Rayan's home, then to Lisa's, on both occasions to "reveal" them as "Laure." The "reveal" itself, I should note, takes place offscreen and the viewer does not hear the mother's explanation nor the reaction of the other parents, in keeping with Sciamma's focus on telling the story "at the height of a child's gaze" (Waldron 2013, 64), as I will discuss in more detail below. The "reveal" between the children's parents and, by extension, from parents to children ultimately leads to the deeply painful scene where Mikaël/

Laure is caught in the forest by the other children who force them to unzip their shorts and oblige Lisa to pronounce a "verdict" on their biological sex. The film ends on the last day of the school holidays. Mikaël/Laure's pregnant mother has given birth to a baby boy and Mikaël/Laure looks down from their apartment to see Lisa looking up. The last images of the film echo the first encounter between the two, as they stand opposite each other, and Lisa asks their name. This time the response is "Laure," followed by the beginnings of a smile, and the end credits run.

As Ricardo Zulueta observed in his review of *Tomboy* for the journal *Film and History*, Sciamma tended to "avoid … acknowledging the queer implications inherent in *Tomboy*" (2012, 108). For Zulueta, the absence of explicit engagement with the film's queerness on the part of its director very much leaves that terrain open for fruitful exploration by viewers, critics, and scholars: "If not the director's focus, then, ours will be to contemplate queer issues such as lesbianism, transsexualism, and homophobia found in *Tomboy*" (2012, 108).

It is worth underlining that Sciamma's direct engagement with all things queer *off*-screen has evolved over the course of the decade since *Tomboy*'s release, and that the absence of the term "queer" from interviews with her at the time reflects the contemporary politico-linguistic backdrop in France. Indeed, while my focus here is absolutely on *Tomboy* as a *queer* classic and on Sciamma as a director of a queer classic, I am nevertheless nervous about the potential erasure of the centrality of lesbian identities, lesbian desires, and lesbian experiences in her work by, in a sense, stepping over the "lesbian" label and moving directly to "queerness." After all, as Clara Bradbury-Rance has argued, at times "the fluid possibilities of queer theory … have threatened to flatten out gender difference, using this lack of difference to shield the lack of availability or interest that in fact makes the lesbian disappear altogether" (2019, 142). In this context, we can understand why it was important to Sciamma, across so many of the interviews around the release of *Naissance des pieuvres*, then *Tomboy*, and then *Bande de filles*, to identify as a lesbian director and to underline lesbian narratives, characters, themes, etc., where they arose in her films, "enabl[ing], rather than flatten[ing] out, the paradoxes inherent in the representation of sexuality, unsettling rather than bolstering its coherence in the visible image" (Bradbury-Rance 2019, 143). There have, of course, been other lesbian French film directors but, in recent decades, it is difficult to think of any who have been as openly so as Sciamma. She has simultaneously and determinedly claimed a place as both lesbian *and* queer filmmaker, thereby demonstrating that "lesbian cinema – in its queer form – has never been more mobile and dynamic" (Bradbury-Rance 2019, 143).[13]

Now, and in particular in the wake of the tremendous success of her 2019 film *Portrait de la jeune fille en feu* (*Portrait of a Lady on Fire*),[14] Sciamma is often referred to, and refers to herself, as a *queer* filmmaker (in both Anglophone and Francophone coverage). However, at the time of *Tomboy*'s release, the term "queer" was not in common usage in the mainstream French press nor in mainstream coverage of French cinema. It was only in 2019 that the editors of the French dictionary *Le Robert* included the word "queer," meaning: "an individual whose sexual orientation does not correspond to the dominant models" (cited in Schmitt 2018). The examples of early usage in French provided via the *La Langue française* website date from the early years of the twenty-first century.[15] That the term has been shifting into more mainstream contemporary usage is also signalled by French radio station France Inter's autumn 2019 launch of a series of podcasts entitled *Intérieur Queer*, the first episode of which was called, quite simply, "C'est quoi, le queer?" or, in English, "What is 'queer'?" In the domain of visual cultures, the Cannes Film Festival's first ever Queer Palm was only awarded in 2010, and while the TV series *Queer as Folk* had been screened with the original English title on Canal+ in 1999, for some (Perreau 2018), the broadcast five years later of a French version of the US show *Queer Eye for the Straight Guy* on TF1 highlighted some of the paradoxes in the evolving usage: "In the French version of the show in 2004, the word 'queer' is used in order not to talk about homosexuality." In this way, Perreau argues, the French TV entertainment industry found a way to target new gay audiences without running the risk of shocking a wider audience.

The specifics of this audiovisual context make more sense if we consider the much broader difficulties particular groups and/or communities encounter when they seek any form of acknowledgment – official or otherwise – in the context of traditional French republicanism. As Denis Provencher asserts: "Traditionally, France has maintained a strong male-centred and hetero-normative presence in both the public and private domains, which has excluded most other forms of citizenship for centuries" (2007, 16). While Article 1 of the French constitution states that "France shall … ensure the equality of all citizens before the law, without distinction of origin, race or religion," in reality, the citizen who is envisaged here is not a blank canvas. Rather, French republicanism "has also created restraints … and public displays of sexual identity have not always been well received" (Gunther 2008, 2). Neither, for that matter, have challenges to a rigid, traditional, binary notion of gendered identities tended to be received as positive engagements with republicanism in its traditional forms.

By way of example, in the early 2010s, not long after *Tomboy*'s release, a series of controversies unfolded in France around revisions to school curricula. Most notably, 2013 saw the launch of a set of educational materials referred to as the ABCD *de l'égalité* (*The Equality* ABC); the aim of this launch was to "combat stereotypes of gender … and to challenge the norms that mean that the sexes adopt specific behaviours, from an early age" (Euzen 2014). It would be difficult to overstate the strength of feeling against this initiative and the threat it was perceived as posing to the very structures of the state. As Camille Robcis explains, parents feared that "their children will be taught homosexuality, masturbation, and transgenderism – and, more broadly, that they will become citizens who embrace nihilism, relativism, radicalism, social constructionism, and all the values they attribute to the 'theory of gender'" (cited in Duong 2014).[16]

Naming and Gendering in Reviews

This complex and, at times, tense relationship between French republicanism and sexual or gendered difference played out in particularly stark ways through the debates around same-sex partnership legislation in the 1990s and 2000s. And in turn these debates came to a head, at least momentarily, with the introduction of the so-called "Mariage pour tous" (Marriage for all) legislation in 2013. Discussion of such social and legislative evolutions is not explicitly a feature of the narrative of *Tomboy*, and yet it is difficult not to assume that the growing intensity of debates on topics related to sexuality, gendered identities, and family structures played out, whether consciously or otherwise, through the language used across reviews of, and articles about, *Tomboy*. Indeed, on its release in 2011, as we will see below, reviewers adopted a range of strategies in relation to the film's central conceit, illustrating the complexities that emerge from a film that is not so much interested in the *drama* of whether "Mikaël" will be "outed" as "Laure," nor in exploring the reasons why Mikaël/Laure might not have offered an alternative to Lisa's initial assumption that she is talking to a new *boy*.[17] Rather, as Sciamma herself describes (in Dokhan 2011), *Tomboy* is interested in *how* Mikaël/Laure acts, in what they do: "It's a film that is centred on action. We're not wondering 'why is she doing that?' but 'how is she doing it?'"[18] Contemporary reviewers were thus faced with an initial choice: in a film where, for the first quarter of an hour or so, the gender of the central character is first unknown, apparently given at the nine-minute mark, then subsequently reinscribed a few minutes later, do you run with the spoiler? And following that decision, the same critics then had to make choices about whether they called the central character "Mikaël" or "Laure" (or both), whether they referred to the central character as a boy or a girl, and so on. And they were making these decisions against a backdrop of heated social, political, and cultural debate on closely related issues.

As most readers will know, French is a gendered language, the significance of which will become obvious through the reviews cited below. That is to say that nouns are given a gender (either masculine or feminine, there is no neuter in French) and that gender determines features of linguistic usage around the noun (for example, adjectival endings usually also mark the gender of a particular term, definite and indefinite articles are also marked in gendered terms, etc.). While debates around rather antiquated stereotypes produced through such rigid linguistic gendering have been going on for decades in France, a series of substantial changes in practice (and associated controversies) have arisen over more recent years. Although an initial government circular was published as early as March 1986 in metropolitan France proposing the "feminization" of job titles, administrative grades, and so on, it was only in 2017 that that became common practice, four decades after such linguistic transformations were being carried out in Quebec.

That year also saw the introduction of the "point médian," the name given to a punctuation mark in the form of a "floating full stop positioned mid-word" that enables the author to include both masculine and feminine forms (de Kervasdoué 2021). By way of example, "les Français" (masculine plural) would traditionally have been the accepted plural to indicate a group of French people, as long as at least one member of that group was male. Even if only one member was male and all other group members were female, the masculine form would be used for the plural. The introduction of the "point médian" allows for the same term to be written as "les *Français·es*" thus including both the masculine plural ending ("s") and the feminine plural ending ("es").

Such linguistic debates may seem rather far removed from cinematic concerns. However, insofar as linguistic usage also determines the "accepted" ways in which stories can be told, where that story is one of complexity and nuance, particularly around questions of gender or gender*ing*, the linguistic limitations play a role. And since *Tomboy*'s 2011 release predated the introduction of the inclusive or gender-neutral language ("écriture inclusive") that has since become increasingly commonplace in French, the linguistic limitations are particularly significant. Contemporaneous reviewers were largely faced with linguistic choices that were still being framed in binary terms.

In response to these dilemmas, an overview of more than a dozen reviews published at the time of the film's release in France shows that critics adopted a number of approaches. Emmanuèle Frois (2011), writing in *Le Figaro*, is among those who chose to adopt a gender-specific stance from the outset, describing the film as the story of Laure who "se fait passer auprès de sa nouvelle bande d'amis pour un garçon" (passing as a boy with her new friends – though, in fact, whereas the English pronominal adjective is gendered in agreement with the speaker, in French its gender depends on the noun to which it refers). Frois does begin to refer to the central character as "l'enfant" (the child) around a third of the way into the review, but only after having set up a binary opposition that literally paints the scene in terms of pink versus blue ("From their physical appearance to their personal or sporting preferences, nothing is pink but rather everything is blue for this child"). Olivier De Bruyn's review in the weekly news magazine *Le Point* takes a similarly rigidly gendered approach and, in his opening paragraph, refers to Laure as "une gamine" (a little girl) and "l'héroïne juvenile" (the young heroine), emphasizing later that Laure is "une très jeune fille" (a very young girl) rather than seeing the film as a consideration of someone on the very cusp of adolescence questioning their gendered identity. Julien Solal, in his review of the film's DVD release for news weekly *L'Express* (2011), not only explicitly genders the central character as female from the opening line onwards ("the film's tomboy is a 10-year-old girl called Laure") but also psychologizes the narrative in ways that are simply not part of Sciamma's approach. Specifically, Solal describes the film as "a forensic study of the psychology of a child who is struggling with her identity." As well as pathologizing Mikaël/Laure, Solal also uses the noun "enfant" in the feminine form, although, as we will see below, alternatives are possible. Even publications that now refer to Sciamma as a queer director opted for a firm assertion of a gender binary; for instance, Jean-Marc Lalanne, writing in *Les Inrockuptibles* (2011), stated that, while audiences may initially have thought the child driving the car was a boy, "we quickly learn that it is a girl."

Others, though, opted to make intelligent, creative use of the possibilities of French grammar, taking advantage of the fact that, even in 2011, before the arrival on the scene of gender-neutral pronouns such as "iel,"[19] there were already ways for reviewers to demonstrate a sensitivity to the issues at hand through the choices they made. In other words, it is possible to "loosen the constraints of French grammar while still remaining within the boundaries of intelligibility" (Kosnick 2019, 159). For example, although French is a gendered language, there are also a very small number of nouns that can be either masculine or feminine without any changes to their spelling. The relevant example in relation to *Tomboy* is the French word for "child" (*enfant*), which can be either masculine or feminine and thus offers a degree of ambiguity that appealed to a number of reviewers. Second, the third-person pronoun "ça" can also, particularly in informal language, be used to refer to an "it" that might conventionally or formally be referred to as "he" or "she." That flexibility *can* also be used disparagingly or insultingly – "ça" as "it" has the same force as "it" can have in English when used to refer to an individual. Nevertheless, "ça" can also offer a way to bypass the gender binary in contexts where other strategies might not be immediately available.[20]

This linguistic flexibility was something that critic Jean-Luc Douin (2011), for instance, writing in *Le Monde*, took advantage of, identifying the central character as "un enfant de 10 ans" (a ten-year-old child – using the masculine indefinite article "un" and gendering terms in the masculine). Douin offered a spoiler alert before explaining how the film's narrative unfolds, but what is particularly interesting in his article is that, although the conventions of French grammar bind him, he is also quick to frame Mikaël/Laure's narrative in terms of choice and the individual's right to choose their own narrative and identity. Douin also points to parallels between *Tomboy* and Sciamma's previous film, *Naissance des pieuvres*, describing both works as explorations of "an apprenticeship of cruelty" and analyses of intolerance of social, sexual, and gendered difference.[21]

Perhaps the more willing a critic is to engage with the complexities of the questions Sciamma explores the more likely it is that they will have also engaged with the specific linguistic complexities of Mikaël/Laure's story. We might argue that this is the case, for instance, in Thomas Baurez's review for *L'Express* (2011): the author uses existing conventions of language and punctuation in order to underline non-fixity: "Laure/Michael[22] a 10 ans. Il/elle nous est présenté(e) dans toute son ambiguïté sexuelle" (Laure/Michael is ten. S/he is presented to us in all of their sexual ambiguity). Baurez explicitly refers to his own strategy in the review, noting, for example, that he will not give the name of the main actor (opting for the term "interprète," which is typically used in its masculine form whether it refers to a male or a female actor) in order to avoid giving anything away.

Gérard Lefort adopts a similar stance in his 2011 review, in *Libération*, where he uses the gender-neutral potential of "enfant" and the conventions of informal French and refers to the central character as "ça." Although more than a decade on, I find myself uncomfortable rereading Lefort's words, I can also see how, in the context of mainstream metropolitan French linguistic conventions of the time, Lefort's "ça" is precisely a means of noting the impossibility of not gendering Mikaël/Laure. No "they" is available here, and Lefort is writing before the advent of non-binary pronouns.[23] Instead, I would argue, Lefort makes use of the conventions available to him in an attempt to place control of the self-narrative in Mikaël/Laure's hands. For example, Lefort first describes Mikaël/Laure's encounter with Lisa and notes: "Ça dit s'appeler Michaël. Comme un garçon" ("They say their name is Michaël. Like a boy") before going on to describe the same child's return home a little later: "Rentré à la maison, Michaël, c'est sa mère qui le dit, c'est Laure. Comme une fille"

("Back home, Michaël is Laure, that's what their mother says. Like a girl." It is also worth noting that the past participle "rentré" is gendered in the masculine singular form here). Talking about Zoé Héran's performance in the role of Mikaël-Laure, Lefort plays further with the rules and conventions of French grammar when he states: "Elle trompe autant qu'il trouble" (she tricks the viewer as much as he troubles the viewer). Ordinarily, as anyone who has ever sat in a classroom learning French will know, a feminine and masculine pronoun (elle/il) cannot both be used to refer to the same object or person.

Lefort's use of the word "tromper" ("to trick" or "to deceive") brings me to another striking feature that emerges if we look back over the 2011 reviews in France and, to an even more pronounced extent, those that followed the film's US release, namely the frequency with which Mikaël/Laure's actions were explicitly framed in terms of deception. Such notions did creep into some of the French-language reviews with, for example, Diatkine (2011) concluding that the film focuses on "secrets that bind siblings together." Jean-Luc Douin (2011) develops the notion more fully as he talks about Mikaël/Laure having been "forced to reveal their sex" or "to *confess* their *true* first name" (the italics are mine). On occasion, the tone of some reviews did make it sound as though the reviewer was offended by Mikaël/Laure's actions – for example, Olivier De Bruyn (2011) suggests that Mikaël/Laure may have decided "on the spur of the moment" to make their friends believe they were a boy "like the others." De Bruyn also claims that Mikaël/Laure was guilty of "an act of deception"[24] (supercherie), "a prisoner [in the feminine form] of her initial lie." De Bruyn's language is striking: instead of taking a more generous or compassionate approach to the situation, the author frames Mikaël/Laure as a deliberate manipulator. The force of De Bruyn's descriptions is even starker here if we consider that, onscreen, we also hear Lisa noting that Mikaël/Laure is not "like the others" – but with a sense of mild curiosity and interest, rather than as an expression of betrayal or concern.

Broadly speaking, French critics who used the lexis of trickery in their reviews tended to do so, not in a directly accusatory fashion, not blaming

Mikaël/Laure for having carried out some kind of unforgivable deception, but rather as a means of foregrounding precisely the kind of existential dilemma the reviewers found *themselves* facing. By contrast, some reviews in the mainstream US press adopted a more overtly critical stance in relation to Mikaël/Laure's choices and actions. Manohla Dargis, for instance, in the *New York Times* (2011), refers to Mikaël/Laure's "lies" and "fibs," Roger Ebert (2012) speaks of a "deception" that must come to an end as the summer holidays draw to a close, and in *The Village Voice* Melissa Anderson (2011) talks of a "gender illusion." Jean-Paul Pryor, writing for *AnOther*, is similarly direct, referring to Laure as "a girl who *tricks* her peers into thinking she's just another one of the boys" (2011; my italics). Nevertheless, just as most French coverage tried to engage with the complexities of the film within the linguistic limitations of the time, so too was Anglophone (US and elsewhere) mainstream coverage of *Tomboy* largely generous and positive. And on both sides of the Atlantic, this coverage can be seen as very much aligned with what Sciamma herself said of the film in the "Director's Statement" included on the European Film Awards website, namely that she constructed it around "a very simple and strong argument, *the story of a lie*" (Sciamma cited in EFA 2011).

Finally, some French reviewers also played with the fact that Sciamma chose to give her film an English-language title (*Tomboy*) rather than using the French term for "tomboy," namely "garçon manqué" which literally translates as "failed boy." While the immediate linguistic reference to "failure" may be absent in the English-language term, "tomboy" nevertheless is a term that comes with its own baggage: "Tomboyism tends to be associated with a 'natural' desire for the greater freedoms and mobilities enjoyed by boys. Very often it is read as a sign of independence and self-motivation … Tomboyism is punished, however, when it appears to be the sign of extreme male identification (taking a boy's name or refusing girl clothing of any type) and when it threatens to extend beyond childhood and into adolescence" (Halberstam 1998, 6). Understandably, Sciamma was asked about the choice of the English-language term in her title and she explained, in no uncertain terms, that she wanted to avoid the negative judgment with which the French term is so clearly imbued. After all, as she said in response to one interviewer, being a tomboy "is something you can be very successful at!" (*Women and Hollywood* 2011).

Against this backdrop, we can perhaps better understand the absence of the term "queer" from much of the press coverage at the time of *Tomboy*'s release, and from interviews with Sciamma. We can also understand that "the discourses and debates emerging from and cohering around *Tomboy* … speak, rather poignantly, to the questions of visibility, representability, legibility, intelligibility and appearance (of sex, gender and sexuality) that the film itself raises and works through" (Lindner 2018, 199). Rather than representing a "decision to discuss her film with the media in an innocuous, non-confrontational tone in order to reach a broader audience," as Zulueta (2012, 110) further suggests, we must also contextualize the film's reception within the French politico-linguistic landscape outlined above, in particular with regard to common usage of the term "queer" in French. We might also note that, in most French reviews and press coverage from 2011–12, the term "trans" or "transgenre" was equally absent. Reviewers, critics, and journalists more often opted to take their lead from Sciamma's own tendency to position the film as an exploration of gender identity, rather than specifically as the narrative of a trans child. Nevertheless, *Tomboy* can also clearly be seen as one of a number of films "that challenge the lack of attention given to the complexity of individuals' identities and the neglect of trans-subjectivities in mainstream representation" (Saunders 2014, 181).

Understandably, some have questioned (and criticized) the absence of the term "trans" in contemporary discussion of the film; on a more positive note, I would nevertheless suggest that we must not overlook the importance of the *presence* of the term "lesbian" in the same press coverage. Nor should we ignore the fact that, since the film was released, as the discussion above maps out, the word "queer" in French has moved from the realm of a largely scare-quote-contained Americanism to an adjective (and a noun, for that matter) in more common and frequent usage. *Tomboy*'s narrative takes us through the shifting sands of childhood onscreen. However, an examination of the changes in media coverage of the film since its release also demonstrates significant shifts in linguistic usage on questions of gender and sexualities in France.

Tomboy: Cast and Crew

To return to *Tomboy*'s production context, the film's small technical crew includes people very closely associated with Sciamma, who relies on many of the same colleagues from film to film. I am thinking here, first and foremost, of producer Bénédicte Couvreur, film editor Julien Lacheray, and musician and composer Jean-Baptiste de Laubier (known as Para One), all three of whom have worked on every film Sciamma has directed to date, from *Naissance des pieuvres* to *Petite Maman* (2021). Lacheray also edited Sciamma's 2010 short film *Pauline*. Sciamma's tight-knit core working crew also includes casting director Christel Baras, who, as well as her role in the production of each of Sciamma's full-length films, has also played small (in terms of screen time) but significant onscreen roles in *Naissance des pieuvres* (as a swimming coach who humiliates Adèle Haenel's Floriane for not having shaved her armpits properly before a competition),[25] *Tomboy* (as the mother of Lisa), and *Portrait de la jeune fille en feu* (as the *faiseuse d'anges* who carries out Sophie's abortion). Crystel Fournier was responsible for cinematography across the "trilogy," and Claire Mathon was the cinematographer for *Portrait de la jeune fille* and *Petite Maman*. Just as we might talk about there being a certain concision and economy in Sciamma's cinematic aesthetic, so too can we understand that that concision and economy start from the building blocks of each of the films.

In terms of the onscreen cast, much was made of the performances by the two central children: Zoé Héran in the role of Mikaël/Laure and Malonn Lévana as their younger sister, Jeanne. According to Sciamma, because of how

Figure 6
Mikaël/Laure and Jeanne.

quickly she wanted the film to be made, she knew that the casting process also needed to be dealt with expediently, and had heard "a rumour" (Dokhan 2011) about Héran: "People told me she was atypical, that she could be androgynous, a little bit of a tomboy, not easy to cast … I thought to myself: that's what I'm after!" Sciamma saw Héran on the second day of casting, and, in her words, "we built the rest around her." The film was shot in the suburb where Héran lived, and the other children in the group of friends were Héran's real-life friends (Dokhan 2011).

Only four adults appear onscreen: Mikaël/Laure and Jeanne's unnamed parents and the mothers of Lisa and Rayan. The latter are both played by members of the crew. Mikaël/Laure and Jeanne's mother is played by Sophie Cattani, whose previous roles had tended to be in TV series or short films. Their father, on the other hand, is played by Mathieu Demy, the son of Agnès Varda and Jacques Demy, who appeared as a child and teen actor in films directed by his mother: *L'une chante, l'autre pas* (*One Sings, the Other Doesn't*, 1977), *Documenteur* (1981), *Kung-fu Master* (1988), and *Jane B. par Agnès V.* (1988), as well as in his father's *Trois places pour le 26* (*Three Seats for the 26th*, 1988), or in the animated film *La Table tournante* (*Turning Table*, co-directed by Jacques Demy and Paul Grimault, 1988). Although Sciamma claims *not* to have chosen Demy on the basis of his cinematic heritage but rather because he represented the type of figure she wanted the father to be in *Tomboy* – "tender, luminous" (Dokhan 2011) – it is nevertheless difficult not to read him as a means of connecting "Sciamma's work to the heritage of feminist and queer filmmaking in France" (Wilson 2021, 52).[26]

Sciamma's Career

Before *Tomboy*, Sciamma had directed one other full-length film (*Naissance des pieuvres*) released in 2007, only two years after she completed her training at the FEMIS film school in Paris, and she directed the eight-minute short film *Pauline* in 2010. Since *Tomboy*'s release in 2011, Sciamma has directed another three full-length films to date: *Bande de filles* (2014, the third film in the loose "trilogy" discussed above); the hugely successful *Portrait de la jeune fille en feu* (2019); and *Petite Maman*, shot during the Covid lockdowns of autumn 2020. Like *Tomboy* a decade before, *Petite Maman* premiered at the Berlinale in 2021. As well as her work as director, Sciamma also has writing credits on a range of films made by other directors – from André Téchiné's *Quand on a 17 ans* (*Being 17*, 2016) to the stop-motion animation *Ma Vie de Courgette* (*My Life as a Courgette*, 2016) directed by Claude Barras via Jacques Audiard's 2021 film *Les Olympiades* (*Paris, 13th District*), which, as further evidence of the concentric circles of Sciamma's filmmaking world, also stars Noémie Merlant of *Portrait* fame. Sciamma's writing credits also include some television work on the supernatural Canal+ series *Les Revenants* (*The Returned*), for example.

Figure 7
Naissance des pieuvres poster.

Figure 8
Jeanne Moreau, Céline Sciamma, and the cast of *Naissance des pieuvres* at the 2008 César ceremony.

From her directorial début with *Naissance des pieuvres*, "based on Sciamma's graduation project" from the FEMIS and "semi-autobiographical in nature" (Smith 2023a, 116), it was clear that she was a director who would go on to make her mark. The film won the French César Award for Best First Film in 2008, which already begins to indicate the impact it made. However, what stands out even more from that ceremony is the point at which Jeanne Moreau, recipient of that year's César d'honneur, summoned Sciamma and "sa jeune équipe" (namely the three female stars of the film: Pauline Acquart, Louise Blachère, and Adèle Haenel)[27] back up to the stage and handed Sciamma the award: "You look after it and you will pass it on from year to year, OK?" Talking about this moment a decade later, Sciamma described the significance of Moreau's gesture, not only in terms of the future of independent French cinema (about which Moreau had spoken during her own acceptance speech) but also because she (Moreau) was entrusting her award to four young women, representatives of a new generation of French filmmakers (see Loop-Sider interview). Sciamma has since given the award to the Moreau Foundation, specifically created in order for them to continue its transmission.

Nevertheless, against this backdrop of success, it is also crucial to address the fact that, while much of the reception of Sciamma's "trilogy," whether academic or popular, has been positive, *Bande de filles* has been received in less uncomplicatedly positive terms, specifically in response to its representation of Black experience by a white, middle-class director. Such critiques are clearly articulated, for example, through the title of Annette Joseph-Gabriel's 2019 article "Who Gets to Speak for Black French People?," where Joseph-Gabriel argues that Sciamma relies "on the images that have come before, on the fixed ideas of the *banlieue*[28] that her audience will bring to the film" and that "*Bande de filles* does little to trouble those fixed ideas." While acknowledging that Sciamma "has no control over what reviewers will say about her film," Joseph-Gabriel further notes that "the exotic, colonialist language arises from the gaze that [Sciamma's] lens invites viewers to adopt."

Mame-Fatou Niang, co-director with Kaytie Nielsen of the 2017 documentary *Mariannes noires*, has also written and spoken about the problematic nature of Sciamma's representation. Indeed, Niang challenges that Sciamma is in a position to offer a representation of young Black women in the *banlieue*. For Niang, while *Bande de filles* is a "magnificent film," it also disturbed her because Sciamma's depiction of her characters is so one-dimensional, presenting them as "cardboard cut-outs": "They are nothing but categories with a violent big brother, a silent mother, an absent father, as though all of that were natural. There is no exploration of what might have shaped these girls. Only what she knows of the *banlieue* went into the film. It reproduces stereotypes and adds nothing" (Niang cited in Barlet 2018). In interviews around the release of *Bande de filles*, Sciamma repeatedly asserted a "universalist" approach to her subject matter, describing her desire "to talk about girlhood universally" (in Zafiris 2015). Contrasting *Bande de filles* with Richard Link-

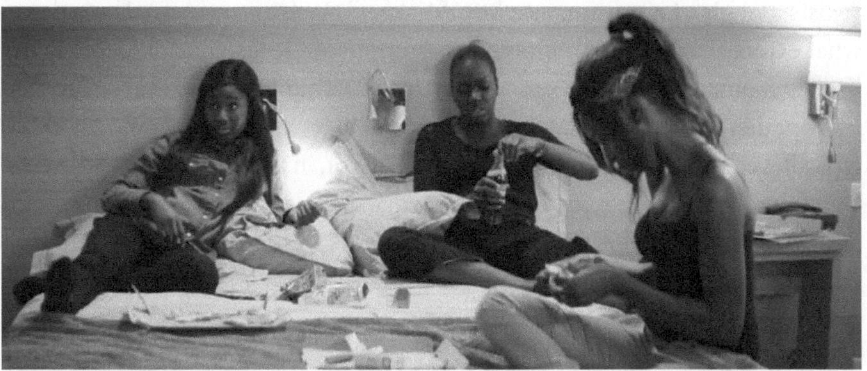

Figure 9
Bande de filles: Hanging out in a hotel room.

later's *Boyhood*, as she was often prompted to do, she noted: "What's universal in America about teenagehood is a middle-class white boy with average dreams. We pick a character at the margins and say what's universal is a 16-year-old black girl" (in *The Independent* 2015).

This statement is very clearly at odds with Mame-Fatou Niang's observation that "before one can universalise the black body, one needs to engage with a whole range of representations … that are projected upon it" (in Barlet 2018). Niang further notes that, while Sciamma spoke about how she "took these girls as blank canvases," such statements erase Black experience insofar as they fail to take account of the fact that "black bodies are not blank canvases: they are entities charged with History."[29] The challenges Joseph-Gabriel, Niang, and others have rightly brought to such assertions of "universalism" have triggered and continue to shape ongoing debates on – and within – French cinema.

My intention here is not to sidestep such criticism. Indeed, I am conscious that similar criticism could be levelled at Sciamma as a cisgender filmmaker delivering a narrative that centres on a "gender non-conformist" child who "exists as a girl, Laure, and as a boy, Mickaël" (Wilson 2021, 59). I wonder to what extent Sciamma's simultaneous claiming of the lesbian and queer labels doesn't ironically serve to "get her off the hook," in the sense that she is seen as empathetic to non-normative perspectives in terms of gender and sexuality, regardless of a lack of specific lived experience of, in this case, a "transidentité." With that in mind, I want to acknowledge the significant criticism of Sciamma's position in directing *Bande de filles* while at the same time recognizing that my own primary focus is on *Tomboy* and its focus on what I see as the queer potential of childhood.

Portrait de la jeune fille en feu and Its Multiple Impacts

Bande de filles was followed, in Sciamma's directorial filmography, by the 2019 historical drama *Portrait de la jeune fille en feu*, whose impact on the contemporary French cinematic – and, indeed, wider cultural – landscape it would be difficult to overstate. *Portrait* garnered tremendous critical acclaim and cemented Sciamma's position as well as that of the film's principal actors, Adèle Haenel and Noémie Merlant, as leading figures in contemporary French sociopolitical debates – particularly on questions of gender and sexualities.

In cinematic terms, *Portrait* represents a dramatic shift in geographical and historical focus for Sciamma. Set in eighteenth-century Brittany, it recounts the relationship between young aristocratic woman Héloïse (Haenel), painter Marianne (Merlant), and the young house servant Sophie (Luana Bajrami). Héloïse is promised in marriage to a suitor in Milan. Her mother (Valeria Golino) commissions Marianne to paint her portrait following her daughter's refusal to sit for the first painter she employed. Marianne's role, though, is initially kept from Héloïse, and she is first introduced to the household as Héloïse's companion. The film explores the relationship between the two as it emerges from covert portraiture, to burgeoning friendship, to collaborative partnership after Marianne reveals the true purpose of her presence, to a sex-

Figure 10
Marianne and Héloïse in *Portrait de la jeune fille en feu.*

ual and romantic relationship that ends when Héloïse's mother returns, to the completion of the portrait and Marianne's departure. While the film certainly charts new historical and geographical territory for Sciamma, its thematic, political, and ethical concerns are very similar to those I have outlined across the "coming of age" trilogy, namely the impact of gendered codes and norms in society, queer desire, and what has come to be termed "the female gaze."[30]

The film's significance, though, did not lie solely in the excitement for queer cinema audiences in seeing Sciamma exploring new ground. Nor was it purely because she was working once more with Adèle Haenel, who had played the role of Floriane in *Naissance des pieuvres* (and provided the voice of the offscreen partner in the short *Pauline*) and with whom Sciamma had subsequently had a romantic relationship. These factors certainly had their role to play, as did the fact that Sciamma spoke openly of *Portrait* having been inspired by her relationship with Haenel (see, for example, Trouillard 2020). What was much more significant in socio-cultural terms was the role that the film, its central cast members, and the director played in a specific moment in the evolution of gender and sexual politics in France and beyond. The film screened at Cannes in May 2019, where it was nominated for the Palme d'Or and won both the Queer Palm[31] and the prize for Best Screenplay for Sciamma. It was released on French screens in September of the same year to rapturous reviews and then released in the US (first in December 2019, then more widely in February 2020) and in the UK (also in February 2020). Its viewing figures outside France were clearly affected by the timing of the release and the outbreak of Covid-19, but to date, it has taken over $10 million at the global box office.

Sciamma, Haenel, and Merlant were omnipresent in most media coverage of the film around its screening at Cannes and thereafter. More often than not, the trio appeared together, completing each other's responses to questions and talking in unerringly positive terms about the collaborative nature of their work on the project. And across those many, many interviews, they spoke of solidarity, trust, desire, and the fun of working in such a supportive environment. Beyond discussions of the film, the director and actors gained media prominence through their actions and statements. In 2013, well before *Portrait* Sciamma had been involved in the founding of Le Deuxième Regard, an organization that campaigned for gender parity in the French film industry. Five years later, in the aftermath of the Weinstein case, the #MeToo movement, and its French counterpart #balancetonporc, she was actively involved in the creation of the Collectif 50/50. This collective was perhaps best known, in its early days, for its interventionist feminist *montée des marches* in Cannes in 2018 when eighty-two international female figures from the world of cinema gathered on the festival's famous red-carpeted staircase and walked up the stairs arm in arm. Cate Blanchett and Agnès Varda led the group, with figures including Sciamma, Marion Cotillard, Salma Hayek, and Kristen Stewart walking together. The significance of the figure eighty-two stems from the fact that, at the time, it represented the number of films directed by women that had been presented in the official competition at Cannes since the festival started in 1946 (Brey 2018). Since then, Sciamma's involvement with the collective has continued, as has her political engagement on issues predominantly related to gender, sexuality, and social justice.

In November 2019, Adèle Haenel participated in a long-form televised interview on Mediapart in which she revealed that she had been sexually abused by French director Christophe Ruggia when she was twelve. Ruggia was arrested in January 2020 and charged with sexual assault of a minor in 2024 (Turchi 2024). When Roman Polanski's name was read out as the recipient of the César for Best Director in February 2020, Haenel stormed out of the televised ceremony shouting "Shame! Shame!" (Une honte, une honte!). Other members of the *Portrait* team followed. During the same ceremony, another French actor, Aïssa Maïga, highlighted the racism of the French film industry when she took to the podium to hand over the award for Best Female Newcomer. As the TV cameras that night showed, it was a speech delivered to a largely sheepish and awkward-looking audience. After the ceremony, she and Haenel made contact, and they featured together on the front page of the French daily newspaper *Libération* in June of the same year under the headline "Finally, something political is happening," with a lengthy joint interview inside (Daumas, Laïreche, and Onana 2020).

Haenel's highly visible political activism has continued through, for example, her involvement with the protest movement to gain justice for Adama Traoré, a young Black French man who died while in police custody in July 2016. Haenel also appeared alongside Nadège Beausson-Diagne on the Mediapart discussion programme *À l'air libre* in November 2020 and they spoke about the so-called "Global Security" law in France,[32] as well as gender-based and racist violence. Haenel and Sciamma marched together as part of the demonstrations for International Women's Day in Paris in March 2020 and again in April 2021 as part of a "Lesbian March" in favour of access to medically assisted fertility treatments for all women and not just those in recognized heterosexual partnerships. What was often striking about these demonstrations on issues related to gender and sexuality was that Haenel and Sciamma[33] not only participated as protestors but *Portrait de la jeune fille en feu* also inspired a wide range of slogans on the placards of their fellow demonstrators: "We are all young ladies on fire!," "More Céline Sciamma, Less Patriarchy" (the rhyme is sadly lost in English – Plus de Céline Sciamma, moins de patriarcat), "Adèle Haenel for President."[34] In 2023, in an open letter published in the weekly magazine *Télérama*, Haenel announced that she was quitting film acting in protest of the profession's "complicity with regard to sexual predators and, more generally, the way in which it collaborates with the racist and ecocidal order of the world" (Haenel 2023).

When French cinemas reopened after lockdown in early summer 2020, there was a huge backlog of unreleased films.[35] Sciamma's fifth feature, *Petite Maman* – the "shooting, editing, and distribution [of which] took place under pandemic conditions" (Lachman 2023, 2016) – was among the films that made their way onto the screens in the first few days after this reopening. Industry magazine *Variety* observed in March 2021 that the film had triggered a "bidding war in multiple territories" and it has gone on to enjoy international releases everywhere from South Korea to Argentina, from Russia to New Zealand, across more than twenty countries to date (Unifrance 2022). The film sees Sciamma return to a quiet observation of childhood, and of girlhood in particular, but in a form alternately described as a "modern fable" (Kermode 2021), "a fairytale" (Fabre 2021; Lussier 2022), and a "classic coming-of-age tale" with "a time-loop spin" (Knight 2021). In *Petite Maman*, Sciamma explores a child's experience of grief through the figure of eight year-old Nelly (Joséphine Sanz), whose grandmother has just died. While her parents are clearing out the grandmother's home Nelly encounters another child, Marion (Gabrielle Sanz), in the woods. That child turns out to be Nelly's own mother and the film's layering and doubling is emphasized by the fact that Nelly and Marion are played by identical twins. As François Massonnat noted in *The*

Figure 11
Petite Maman.

French Review, "the connections with *Tomboy* are immediately apparent," whether in the minimalist scale of the film, its very small cast (eight characters in total), or its depiction of "children left to their own devices who take advantage of relative freedom … in order to explore their existential concerns" (2022, 284).

Thus, from the positive reception of *Naissance des pieuvres* in 2007, through to the critical and popular success of *Portrait* in 2019, right up to her most recent work, Sciamma's films have all made their mark on the French cinematic landscape. They challenge existing visions of gender and sexuality onscreen and off. And Sciamma has also made an important impact through political engagements such as those mapped out above.

Structuring *Tomboy*: Framing and Gazing

It is difficult not to have a backdrop of feminist and queer political activism in mind when (re-)watching *Tomboy* in the early 2020s. And yet this particular queer classic also paved the way for much of what has followed in the intervening decade. In production terms, as I have already noted, it is a small-scale and contained work, as is evident in the size of its cast and crew, its length (82 minutes), and its relatively small budget (an estimated $1 million, according to IMDb). It is tightly contained and focused in its structure, demonstrating "the rigour of a classic tragedy through a unity of space, time and action" (Diatkine 2011).

Sciamma engaged explicitly with the question of the gaze in interviews when the film was released, not only in terms of having sought to avoid the gaze of an adult looking *down* on children or reflecting nostalgically on childhood but also considering Mikaël/Laure's place within a network of gazes (Dokhan 2011). "The character is observing, they are watching the others and trying to act as they do. As a result, there is a multiplication of gazes turned towards the group."[36] From the earlier discussion, it should be clear that the film's *linguistic* framing of its core concerns is significant and that there is much scope for interesting analysis of contemporary attitudes to gender in France via close readings of the linguistic choices of reviewers. However, the film's use of framing in a more conventionally understood *cinematic* register is also crucial – a topic to which I now turn.

First and foremost, in many ways, the film is shot at what we might describe as "child height." In fact, the phrase (or variations on it) recurs across articles and interviews published around the film's release[37] as well as in more recent engagements with Sciamma's work – featuring, for instance, as the title of Audrey Jeamart's *Critikat* interview with Sciamma[38] and in Steph Green's account of the film on the *Screen Queens* website (2019). Sciamma makes repeated strategic use of fixed camera angles to create a frame that makes space for the children as they run, play, dance, swim, and fight, as well as in their moments of calm. Adults must almost bend to fit into this cinematic space, as "the image-track barely leaves the children" (Waldron 2013, 64). It is by no means unusual for us to see the children from head to toe and, crucially, they are almost always on the move – the frame waits for their arrival or return. The rare adults who inhabit their world are filmed from the waist up or in close-up, for example the children's parents leaning against the kitchen surfaces as they prepare and eat dinner or Rayan and his mother framed in the doorway of the family's home. Adults also tend to be filmed standing, sitting, or, in the case of Mikaël/Laure's mother, lying down on her bed in the final stages of pregnancy for most of the film. In other words, the children are the active participants in the narrative, while the adults become almost part of the décor.

For Sciamma, there is a further deliberate choice here in the decision not to film with a handheld camera, running around after the children, but instead to consciously construct a frame: "I wanted there to be a mise en scène, a frame" (Dokhan 2011). In the same interview, Sciamma commented that it is incredibly difficult to film an adult and a child together, acknowledged that the adults look like giants in the film, and said that was one of the reasons why the mother is almost always filmed lying down. As Sciamma further notes, though, her desire to "avoid a nostalgic or introspective adult gaze" on childhood (Jeamart 2011) and to go with the dynamism that emerges from allowing the children to run off in different directions – in the play sequences, for example – should not be interpreted as meaning that the children were in charge of the narrative. Quite the opposite, in fact: from Sciamma's perspective, the use of the static camera forces the children "to exist in the universe you have constructed for them .... The more children there are in the frame, the more authoritarian the mise-en-scène" (Jeamart 2011).

For some critics, this decision nevertheless detracted from the film's success, specifically its ability to appeal to an adult audience. Writing for *Critikat*, for example, Frédéric Caillard (2011) describes "the viewer who may quite legitimately seek a mature perspective on what is at stake in the film and regret the lack of fleshing out from which the characters of the 'parents' suffer."

However, as I have noted above, Sciamma never wants to approach her subject from the perspective of an adult contemplating childhood.[39] Rather, she quite explicitly gives space to the child protagonists, both temporally and physically, to allow the events to unfold at *their* pace and from *their* perspective, with all that that entails – for example, eschewing the more customary tension of the "reveal" in narratives recounting the experiences of gender non-conforming adults or children.

What is striking is not only that Sciamma does not adopt a viewpoint observing the children from adult height. Instead she places the child quite literally in a more elevated position. We have already discussed the film's opening shots when Mikaël/Laure and their father are driving to the new apartment, the latter guiding the former in their experimental driving of the family car. However, before we see Mikaël/Laure at the wheel, the very first shots of them we see are of the shoulders and the back of their head, sticking out through the car's sunroof, and their hand trailing through the air as they drive along. The father's first words to his child are: "Are you alright up there?" Similarly, when Mikaël/Laure first sees the other children, it is from the vantage point of the apartment, looking down on the green space outside the apartment block. As the film draws to a close, after the mother has dragged them to Lisa's and Rayan's homes to tell them that Mikaël is Laure, Mikaël/Laure once more looks down from the balcony and this time sees Lisa gazing upwards at them.[40]

We notice that Mikaël/Laure is not "grounded," not anchored conventionally to their lived environment in such shots, all the more so when we contrast them with two early sequences where the camera films Jeanne's legs from mid-thigh down. Jeanne's feet in particular seem strangely firmly grounded on the apartment floor. I say "strangely" firm here because Jeanne is a smaller, younger child and yet her body seems more confident in its relationship with itself and with its environment. This is the case, for instance, when she has the apparently total absence of self-consciousness that allows her to perform her own dance routine to Mikaël/Laure's musical accompaniment. This brief

Figure 12
Mikaël/Laure at the wheel.

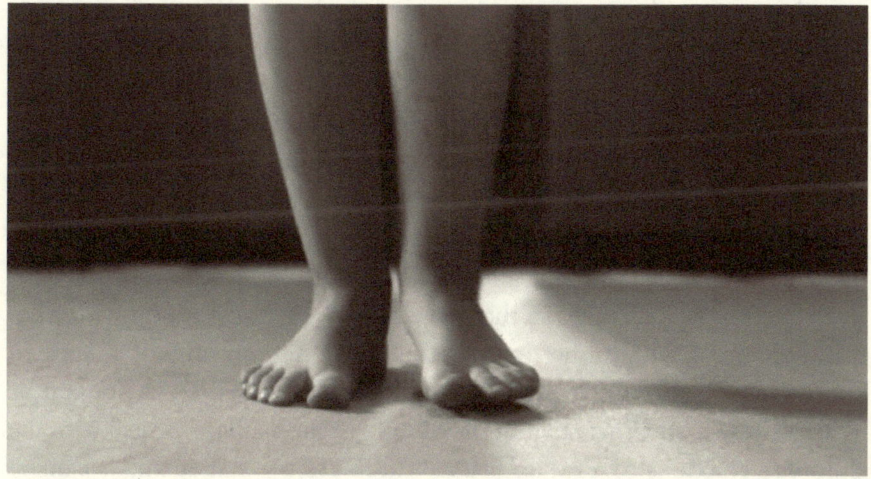

Figure 13
Jeanne's feet.

dance routine will become all the more striking retrospectively when we contrast it with Mikaël/Laure's initially rather reluctant dancing at Lisa's instigation later in the film. The odd angles at which we initially see Mikaël/Laure in relation to the world – upper body poking through the car sunroof or bare legs dangling out through the balcony railings – can be read as instances of Sciamma "allowing the oblique to open up another angle on the world," using the unpredictability of the geometry of Mikaël/Laure's position in the world as a sort of "disorientation device" (Ahmed 2006, 172) that signals a queering of childhood.

We might also see here a visual echoing of the work of Kathryn Bond Stockton, who describes the development of "the queer child" as an example of "sideways growth": "the child who by reigning cultural definitions can't 'grow up' grows to the side of cultural ideals" (2009, 13). In this regard, though, I find that Ahmed's phenomenological approach offers a more helpful framework; indeed I would argue, with Waldron, that "in Stockton's book, sideways growth is often understood retrospectively [... whereas] Laure's gender nonconformity in *Tomboy* ... unfolds in the present" (2013, 63).

It is also worth noting that Sciamma plays not only with the construction of the spatial frame within which the children evolve, but also with the temporal dimensions of the frame in order to make it suit the behaviours and attitudes of her child actors. What I mean by this is that, as she discussed in a number of interviews, rather than filming short scenes and multiple takes of the same short scene, stopping and starting for each take, Sciamma opted instead to use very long takes so that the children could just get on with what they were doing without her interrupting them. Actions might be repeated but the camera continued to shoot. Any individual scene might not appear in its entirety in the final cut, but neither did Sciamma have to deal with the children's reactions to a rather brutal "Cut! Let's try that again!" (Jeamart 2011). In the scene where Mikaël/Laure and Jeanne are playing with Play-Doh, for instance, Sciamma recounts that the children really did play together with

Figure 14
Mikaël/Laure through the sunroof.

the Play-Doh for half an hour and the film crew "took what they needed" from the footage (Jeamart 2011). This level of care and concern is worth noting.

These questions of angle also foreshadow the horizontal framing that Sciamma uses in *Portrait de la jeune fille en feu* where the hierarchies that are thus flattened, at least for the duration of the film, are not between adult and child but between aristocratic woman, independent female painter, and female servant. There, too, Sciamma subverts our expectations of angles and perspectives, and plays with occasional forays into verticality and its potential for constructing or reinforcing traditional power dynamics, only to challenge them by repeated use of wide, horizontal *tableaux*. In these tableaux, for example, we see aristocrat, painter, and servant prepare a meal together, each with their own role to play, their own contribution to make, cleaning

Figure 15
Héloïse, Marianne, and Sophie preparing for mealtime.

and preparing mushrooms, slicing bread, pouring wine, or, in the case of Sophie and in an up-ending of the hierarchy, embroidering as the others prepare the food.[41]

To return to *Tomboy*: just to be clear, oblique or unusual angles to the world never position Mikaël/Laure above other characters as a way to distance them or emphasize a sense of alienation or marginalization specifically related to their gender. Instead, in each case, the view of the world from Mikaël/Laure's momentarily elevated vantage point is immediately preceded or followed by an act of inclusion, of sharing, of burgeoning solidarity. We see this in the shape of parent and child driving the car together and with Mikaël, and then Laure, taking the first steps in a developing friendship and being invited to join with others via Lisa's request to hear their name at the beginning and the end of the film. The repeated use of "disorientation," which forces us to focus in order to understand a relationship between child and world, serves to queer the narrative of childhood we are watching unfold.

Chapter 2

Choreographies of Childhood

Writing about the "coming-of-age trilogy" with a particular focus on *Tomboy* and *Bande de filles*, Katharina Lindner underlined the "bodily tendencies, gestures and modes of embodiment" so often at play in Sciamma's work (2018, 195). In this chapter I explore these further in relation to *Tomboy*, and examine a series of scenes in which we see Mikaël/Laure playing with other children. Sometimes they are indoors; other times they're in the family's apartment, with their sister Jeanne; and sometimes we see them with the wider group of friends outside or in and around the apartment block. These encounters between a child and the environment, between a child and their peers, between a child and their own body offer the viewer insight into the ways in which these children inhabit the world.

Obviously, there is nothing particularly surprising or innovative about the fact that a film *about* childhood would include scenes of children at play. Nevertheless, Sciamma's determination to recount the story at child height means that, rather than just including a handful of scenes of children playing, she largely constructs the film around them. It is this sense of "construction" that underpins my reference to Sciamma's "choreographies" of childhood. As I noted earlier, Sciamma's approach to filming the children in *Tomboy* involved the use of long takes that gave the children the space and the time within which to act but also just be. This allowed for a degree of spontaneity of action

Figure 16
Swimming trip.

on their part. However, that spontaneity was counterbalanced, as Sciamma acknowledged, by the fact that the key turning points and tensions of the narrative were clearly set out in the screenplay and most of the dialogue was written rather than improvised.[1] She did not tell the children precisely where and how to move, or to play, in advance of a scene. Instead she speaks of having "repeatedly entered the frame," of having spoken to the children, and in the case of the bathtub scene, of having added specific bath toys to the set after the younger child referred to them (Jeamart 2011). In this sense, we can understand Sciamma as offering "choreographies" of childhood.

Indoor and Outdoor Loci of Childhood

What's more, Sciamma makes almost exclusive use of what I would describe as the loci of childhood as backdrops to these choreographies: bedrooms, bathrooms, football pitches, the forest. After all, "childhood happens at home, in playgrounds, in classrooms or in the fantasy worlds of a child's ambition" (Hemelryk Donald, Wilson, and Wright 2018, 9). And yet, because Sciamma keeps the children determinedly in the foreground with the adults floating on the periphery – and, indeed, absent from large swathes of the film – we are not in a domain here where "fantasy and desire are ... tied into the worlds of children through the imaginaries that they enable, even as they compete with the intersecting and demanding worlds of adults" (9). Even where action unfolds against a physical backdrop that we might associate more readily with "adult life" – such as, for instance, the driving seat of a car or a kitchen where a family dinner is being prepared – those settings are co-opted into a child-centred perspective, in which play is frequently the dominant mode of expression and engagement.

The driving seat of the car, as we have already seen, is occupied not solely by a grown-up at the wheel but by a grown-up with a child on his lap and with that child, at least partly and definitely joyfully, in control of the car. The kitchen seems small, lively, and cluttered, not only with objects and people fighting for space within the bustling frame but with the competing conversations and exchanges that will be familiar to many viewers. In the (aural) background, Mikaël/Laure and Jeanne's parents discuss schedules and plans and the impact the father's new job routine is likely to have on parental activities with the children. From a brief, concerned glance in their parents' direction, we understand that Mikaël/Laure is aware of the content of their conversation, but the tension is dissipated almost as quickly as it emerges when their father, leaning against the kitchen surface, eating pasta, calls for the children's attention to get them to watch as he tugs on his earlobe

Figure 17
Spaghetti games.

and comically sucks up a strand of spaghetti. In other words, even where the settings lend themselves to a stepping back from the child to allow for an adult perspective, a grown-up interlude where the children's actions or behaviours might be presented as something requiring adult interpretation, Sciamma subverts our expectations. It is the child who remains centre stage. The concerns of a world of grown-ups dissolve into the lives led by the child protagonists.

The key exception comes, of course, in the final section of the film when, as I have already discussed, Mikaël/Laure's mother takes them to their friends' apartments to "reveal" themselves as "Laure." The child has little choice but to obey in these scenes. There is certainly no space for play or imagination in the "reveal." However, even here, Sciamma retains her child-height approach insofar as we do not see or hear the exchanges between Mikaël/Laure's mother and the mothers of the other children. Those conversations take place off-

Figure 18
Mikaël/Laure and Rayan.

screen while Mikaël/Laure is left standing alone. There are no half-heard whispers, no gasps of surprise from another room. Rayan stands next to Mikaël/Laure, wordless, stealing a glance from the corner of his eye. Lisa returns home while Mikaël/Laure's mother is talking to her mother and they call her into the room. When she emerges, she enters the frame in which Mikaël/Laure stands and faces them, as silent as Rayan had been. Lisa then turns and leaves for her own room. Lisa's departure triggers that of Mikaël/Laure, who runs out the apartment door, leaving it swinging open in their haste. No space for play and yet even here we are reminded that this is a narrative of children and of childhood. Although not transformed through play, the spaces around what we imagine to be tense conversations between adults remain spaces governed by the interaction between children.

However, these offscreen confrontations only arise in the film's latter stages. By setting the film during the school holidays, Sciamma sidesteps the school as the most common site of interaction for a group of children of roughly the same age or for potential conflict between children and figures of authority. Instead, the children's sunny days revolve around the football pitch, the forest, and the lake when they are outdoors, and their family home – most often in their bedrooms and bathroom – when they are indoors. I now turn to these settings before examining the choreographies of childhood that unfold across them later in this chapter.

Kitchens, Living Rooms, Hallways: Shared Domestic Spaces

The film is roughly split between one-third indoor settings and two-thirds outdoor, but it is the former that I want to examine most closely. This is not to dismiss the significance of the outdoor locations. Indeed, the forest, as well as coming with the imaginative baggage of fairy tales and horror stories, is clearly laden with meaning for Sciamma, a backdrop from which most social markers were absent but that offers the potential to create an almost "timeless" (Dokhan 2011) depiction of childhood.[2] In *Tomboy*, the forest is a space of shadows and light, the sun rippling through the leaves, a universe cut off from the world of adults (the latter are entirely absent from the forest). It is a space where Mikaël/Laure thinks they will be "safe" to hide away from the other children to pee but also where one of those other children stumbles across them and hollers to inform the others that they have, in fact, wet themselves. It is the space from which, after having been "outed" as Laure by their mother, Mikaël/Laure observes the other children as they chat – but where the sound of a twig breaking is enough to attract the attention of those same children, who chase Mikaël/Laure deeper into the forest and ultimately force them into an emotionally violent gender "reveal." Indeed, Sciamma has noted that she was interested in the idea of a threat that could be built through work on the forest soundscape: "When you're alone in the forest, you're really alone" (Dokhan 2011), a rather unexpected echo of the famous *Alien* tagline "In space no one can hear you scream" (Ridley Scott, 1979). The forest is a space that gives the children an opportunity to play by their own rules with both positive and negative consequences. The supervisory, controlling gaze of adults is absent, but that also means the potential protection that might, under some circumstances, be afforded by that same gaze is likewise absent.

However, I argue that the indoor spaces are similarly integral, and while the forest setting will be discussed in the context of the action that unfolds against it at numerous points, I would like to take some time here to explore a number of the film's key indoor and domestic settings. It should be clear to the viewer from our first glimpse of the family's new home that this is a narrative in which children will be given the opportunity to take the lead. We see this, first and foremost, in the fact that it is Mikaël/Laure who we watch meandering from room to room, casually inspecting their new home, rather than them being directed to their new room by a watchful parent (which could be understood as implying that only their room belongs wholly to them). Quite the opposite. Before Mikaël/Laure inspects what will become their bedroom, they first drift through the family living room and central hallway, taking stock of the full extent of their new environment. In other words, the children's existence is not contained to their own rooms but rather spills out across all the spaces of their home and they are not reliant on parental permission for this to occur. Jeanne and Mikaël/Laure do have their own rooms, spaces that reflect their own interests and tastes, as we quickly learn via a reference to the cuddly toys on Jeanne's shelves in her predominantly pink and white room and, when Mikaël/Laure finishes their inspection of the new home, the mother's enquiry as to what they think of their room and her observation that the blue walls are what Mikaël/Laure wanted.

As well as having their own spaces, though, we also see them in each of the other rooms, whether those we might consider as communal (the kitchen, the bathroom, the living room) or those that, in other films on childhood, might be depicted as being in some sense forbidden territory, like the parents' bedroom. There is no forbidden territory here, no hiding under parents' beds

Figure 19
Mikaël/Laure's hand.

or in wardrobes. Children are not "trespassing" onto adult territory. Instead, Mikaël/Laure drifts into the parents' room and sits on the bed with their mother. They are quickly joined by the father, who carries a giggling Jeanne in his arms and then playfully dumps her on the bed. The camera observes the scene of family unity through the bedroom door.

As well as the brief spaghetti-eating scene mentioned earlier that takes place in the kitchen, significant indoor scenes also unfold in the living room, in the bathroom, and in both children's bedrooms. I will discuss each of these below, but it is also worth noting that Sciamma's vision of the family home does not only make use of the defined, enclosed spaces of individual rooms. Instead, she also makes use of the more liminal domestic spaces. I am thinking specifically here of the corridors and doorways of the apartment, on the one hand, and of its small balcony, on the other. It is not a large apartment, but Sciamma's use of doorways to create frames within frames through which we observe the family together also creates an illusion of distance, reminding us of our position as observers. These doorways and corridors stand in sharp contrast to the expansive and at times chaotic outdoor spaces of the forest, the lake, and the children's other play areas, "the unregulated arenas of childhood" (English 2019, 38). We can, of course, see this as a reminder of an indoor-outdoor, private-public division that is particularly significant in shaping Mikaël/Laure's existence.

It would be fair to say that there is a potential paradox in this nuanced narrative that avowedly steers away from "psychologizing" Mikaël/Laure's actions, decisions, and motivations, on the one hand, while still sustaining a comparatively clear-cut and apparently binary division between "Laure" indoors and "Mikaël" outdoors, on the other. On one reading, it appears to be the case that, as long as the division remains "airtight," Laure can exist indoors and Mikaël outdoors. In other words, "Laure" and "Mikaël" are presented as two distinct identities that we can understand as being distinguishable in gendered terms, i.e., a boy (Mikaël) outdoors, with other children, and a girl (Laure) indoors, with family.

On another reading, though, while Sciamma does make use of distinctly public and private spheres, I would also point out that she makes significant use of the "in-between" spaces of the children's lives – not in the sense that it is in such spaces that significant acts of passing or, indeed, challenges to passing occur, but rather as a reminder that the public/private, indoor/outdoor division is *not* airtight. Indeed it is, in some sense, rather arbitrary. I am thinking here of the car in the film's first shots and, specifically, of the (at that point) unnamed child who is not fully inside the car but rather half in, half out. I am also thinking, though, of the stairwell in the apartment block where Lisa sits waiting for Mikaël/Laure to join her and where, in line with earlier comments about Mikaël/Laure being shown at an unexpected angle to the environment, the latter appears feet first, bounding down the stairs to join a static, seated Lisa. I also have in mind the concrete walkways and landings of the semi-outdoor sections of the apartment block where the kids gather and play Truth or Dare, a game that culminates with Mikaël/Laure having to chew Lisa's pre-masticated piece of gum. It is along these concrete walkways that we see Mikaël/Laure walking home from Lisa's house in a scene I will return to in the next chapter or being dragged to Rayan and Lisa's homes by their mother. It *is* a film that makes distinct use of indoor and outdoor settings, which pushes us to notice what happens indoors and what happens outdoors, but it is simultaneously a film of the in-between spaces of everyday lives.

Returning to the indoor spaces, though, we meet the family as they finish moving into their new home early in the holidays from school that run for two months through July and August in France. We watch as they settle into the new apartment, taking physical ownership of its internal geography, and we are privy to some of the final stages of a house move. The kitchen, as we have seen, serves as a shared space, with the children seated at a table that is positioned centre-frame and the parents on the periphery, at the sink, and leaning against the work surface. The living room is another important shared space in the new apartment, although its importance is not measured in terms of screen time. Only a handful of minutes are spent in it over the duration of the film, split between two scenes, but each of them helps us to understand the quiet calm of the family dynamic, and the second scene highlights the relationship between Mikaël/Laure and their father.

Both scenes take place in the evening. In the first, all four family members are assembled in the living room and seem calmly content in each other's company without any direct exchange taking place. In fact, each person is caught up in their own activity, the children on the floor and the parents sprawled out on the sofa. The father is on his laptop; the mother is reading; Jeanne sits on the floor and plays with toys; and Mikaël/Laure is lying on the floor, picking at strands of thread from the rug. There is no drama, no tension, no conversation. Instead, the scene underscores the banality of the family's existence. In the second living room scene, Mikaël/Laure and their father are playing the Happy Families card game. This time it is the father who sits on the floor while the child has taken ownership of the sofa. The father is sipping beer from a bottle. Mikaël/Laure seems interested and is allowed to try a mouthful, which provokes similar grimaces to the earlier game of Truth or Dare when they had to chew Lisa's gum. The scene draws to a close as Mikaël/Laure flops their head sleepily onto the sofa and starts to suck their thumb, a reminder that the courage and determination of their "passing" is coming from a child. Their father comments that it is unusual to see them sucking their thumb and jokes about how strange that feels if you try it again as an adult – again reminding us that the individual whose experiences we are following is still a child. The concluding frames of the scene emphasize that reminder as the father picks up the child and holds them, rocking to and fro, until Mikaël/Laure seems to fall asleep.

Bathrooms: Mirror, Bathtub, and Make Believe

Although these scenes in the kitchen and the living room tell us something about the family dynamic, the two key indoor sites – particularly in relation to Mikaël/Laure's identity and experience of self – are the bathroom and the children's bedrooms. It is against the tiled and reflective surfaces of the former, during Jeanne and her sibling's shared bath time, that we first hear the mother call the child we have been introduced to as "Mikaël" only five or so minutes earlier (during the outdoor conversation with Lisa) "Laure." While the scene when we hear the mother's disembodied voice[3] shout to "Laure" to hurry up in the bath and then see the child emerging from the bath water, naked, is clearly an important moment, so is the giggling, playful bathing sequence that precedes it. We join Jeanne and Mikaël/Laure at bath time, the pair sitting in the tub, facing each other, framed from the mid-chest upwards. Jeanne is

Figure 20
Mikaël/Laure and Jeanne's bath-time.

singing and we only hear a couple of lines of the song, something about a young girl who falls in love with a boy who plays rock 'n' roll, before the action moves on to a mock press interview of Jeanne as a young star.

However, before I examine that section of the scene, I would like to return to the apparently anodyne song. What we hear is, in fact, a snippet from a rather strange French children's song called "Anatole, Monsieur Paul" whose lyrics, before the lines we hear in the film, include a reference to "girls having style," with their large green eyes, while the boys are described as "big pigs who lift up our skirts." In *Tomboy* we hear the lyric: "She fell in love with a rock and roll boy." The heteronormativity of the song's gender and sexual stereotyping is startling.[4] I should note that the song is not especially well known, and things move quickly in this scene, so even for French viewers the lyrics could well pass by unnoticed. However, in light of what happens next,

I strongly suggest that Sciamma is reminding us of the existence of the clearly gendered codes and conventions that form part of the world beyond the film – the extra-diegetic universe within which we are to imagine that these characters live out the rest of their lives.

I say this because what happens next is that Mikaël/Laure takes the shower head and transforms it into a make-believe microphone and proceeds to interview Jeanne. To do so, Mikaël/Jeanne deepens their voice *and* addresses Jeanne as "Madame," thus doubly underlining a gender binary between would-be interviewer and would-be celebrity. As with the snippet from "Anatole, Monsieur Paul," the interview takes up only a small portion of the bath scene, but the two taken together – with their implicit reminders of gendered codes and conventions – coming as they do just before the children's mother calls Laure's name, rather serve to refocus our minds on the very questions of identity formation Sciamma so often places at the heart of her narratives. The mother's shouted instruction that "Laure" should hurry up not only "reveals" gender through the name but also because it is followed onscreen by the child who had, thus far, been filmed from mid-chest upwards, sitting in the bathtub, as they stand up to get out of the bath. They are framed at full height, naked, for a matter of seconds before wrapping a towel around their body and stepping out of the tub.

However brief this glimpse of Laure/Mikaël naked might be, it is striking that, while it is barely mentioned in French-language reviews of the film,[5] some English-language reviewers seemed shocked and, in some instances, incensed by the fleeting glimpse of a child's genitalia, perhaps echoing Emma Wilson's initial concern that "the scene raises questions about showing any bare children on film, and about the laying bare of trans and queer bodies" (2021, 49). One particularly stark example can be found in the *Irish Times* review that accuses Sciamma of "flirt[ing] with pre-teen nudity" and asks whether there is "some hypocritical comfort to be derived from knowing a lady film-maker shot the scenes depicting a naked 10-year-old?" (Brady 2011).

This is, I would emphasize, an extreme example, but Brady is certainly not alone in highlighting this scene in her review. In contrast, for French journalists, it was more a case of asking Sciamma how she shot the scene, what ethical considerations she took into consideration, and so on (Dokhan 2011; Jeamart 2011). To return to the scene itself, in light of what happens in the final third of the film, once their mother has discovered that "Laure" is also "Mikaël," we can also reflect on the difference between the violence and cruelty that will be imposed through the verbal "reveal" of "Mikaël" as "Laure" by their mother and the visual "reveal" forced upon them by the other children and the safety of this first, brief "reveal" in the bathroom. Indeed, to return to Wilson's initial concern expressed above, rather than focusing on anxiety at the "laying bare," we can instead understand the scene as affirmative, "pursuing Sciamma's deliberate questioning of gender," reminding us that "the trans boy or queer girl body need not be read … as a site of lack or loss" (2021, 49).

There follows the first (and shortest) of a number of brief "mirror-rehearsal scenes" (English 2019, 38). Mikaël/Laure steps out of the bath and catches sight of themselves in the bathroom mirror as they look down at their own chest and dry themselves. In later examples of such scenes, we will see Mikaël/Laure looking in the bathroom mirror for longer, twisting and turning to be able to get a better view of particular parts of their body (chest, shoulders, biceps). We also see them using the mirror inside their wardrobe in a similar way – as a means of checking or assessing their own appearance. This first example lasts but a matter of seconds. There are no words, and we have no access to the child's internal monologue, neither here nor elsewhere in the film, for that matter. However, we understand that what we are witness to is a profound consciousness and questioning of their own body and consideration as to whether they are likely to "pass" in their interactions with the other children. We also understand that "the mirror scenes serve … not only as moments of rehearsal, but also as important moments where Laure can *recognise* themself as Mikaël and can, therefore, truly embody a new gender identity" (English 2019, 38–9).

Figure 21
The haircut.

The bathroom serves as a similarly significant site later in the film, around the fifty-minute mark, when, again, Jeanne and Mikaël/Laure are alone there. This time, the scene occurs after Jeanne has become aware that her sibling is passing as Mikaël outside the family home. On this occasion, the pair are not in the bath but in front of the bathroom sink and mirror, where Jeanne is trimming Mikaël/Laure's hair. Mikaël/Laure is concerned that Jeanne should not trim off too much to ensure that their mother does not notice the change. And they want Jeanne to be careful to cut it straight. Jeanne is affronted at the very notion that she might do otherwise. After the brief exchange about hair length, Mikaël/Laure picks a small tuft of hair out of the sink and places it delicately on their top lip like a moustache, turning to face Jeanne, who guffaws. The giggles intensify as Mikaël/Laure addresses Jeanne, putting on a deeper voice than usual, "Bonjour, Madame," and the pair continue to mess about together, Jeanne trying to copy her elder sibling's moustache but not managing to keep the tufts of hair in place on her top lip.

Like the showerhead interview scene earlier, this is a game that will be very recognizable to many of the film's viewers, and I argue that its purpose is twofold. First, it reminds us of the existence of gendered models and that, although we do not see them interacting with a world beyond their home and play areas, Jeanne and Mikaël/Laure are, of course, aware of those models and codes. Second, though, it also reminds us that, as well as being a story that centres on an individual gender non-conforming child, this is also a story about childhood and children's experiences of childhood more generally. This dual positioning could also be seen as Sciamma hedging her bets, opting not to frame *Tomboy* explicitly and exclusively as the story of a trans child but rather to stay within the arguably less clear-cut narrative frame of childhood investigations of gendered identities in a broader sense. I can absolutely see the argument and the criticism here and certainly, reflecting on the film as a Queer Film Classic more than a decade after its release, in a context in which trans*phobia* does not hedge its bets, I can see why a more definitive positioning from Sciamma would have been welcome. However, I would also argue that seen within the context of the trilogy and the similar refusal of categorical and static definitions (whether of lesbian, bisexual, trans …) across *Naissance des pieuvres*, *Tomboy*, and *Bande de filles*, the film's refusal to use labels is itself a queering strategy.

Bedrooms in *Tomboy*: Who Am I?

Just as the family bathroom becomes a site where gendered codes can be explored, reinforced, challenged, and subverted, so too does the film, in its indoor sequences, make extensive use of bedrooms to similar ends. In many ways, Sciamma is tapping into well-established cinematic conventions here with children's bedrooms and *girls'* bedrooms in particular featuring frequently as key settings in films about childhood, as well as having given rise to their own critical literature analyzing their broader cultural significance, starting with Angela McRobbie and Jenny Garber's "Girls and Subcultures" (1976). As Mary Celeste Kearney noted in her more recent reconsideration of

McRobbie and Garber's work, its publication heralded the arrival of the bedroom as "occup[ying] a privileged place in girl-centred media and cultural studies" (2007, 126).

Given Mikaël/Laure's gender non-conformity, we are clearly not uncomplicatedly dealing with a "girl's" bedroom in *Tomboy*. Then again, some of the action also takes place in both Jeanne and Lisa's bedrooms. Because the family has just moved in, Jeanne's and Mikaël/Laure's bedrooms are not merely backdrops but also topics of conversation; both children are given the opportunity, at different points, to express an opinion on their new room. Jeanne's bedroom primarily features as a play space and somewhere where we are reminded of just how young she is. In one sequence, for example, the siblings are laughing, tickling each other, and playing on Jeanne's bed, with Mikaël/Laure teasing Jeanne and telling her that she smells. This serves to remind us from the outset that childhood is a multi-sensory experience and offers Sciamma an early opportunity to highlight the fact that we are observing *experiences* of the sensations of childhood as we will explore in the final chapter where I examine the film's use of textures.

While Mikaël/Laure and Jeanne are shown living their lives in each of the rooms of the new apartment and as individuals with every right to inhabit the full domestic space, the former's bedroom does, nevertheless, retain a particular status. It is very clearly a space that is largely their own, where they are left to their own devices – until the eruption of tension in the film's final quarter. Indeed, the very fact that it seems to be Mikaël/Laure's own space at the heart of the home underlines the brutality of the interruption that comes the morning after the parents learn Laure is also Mikaël, when their mother wakes them up. As is often the case with Sciamma, there are layers to peel back in this apparently simple scene before we get to the physical and psychological violence of the mother's actions.

The previous evening, as we have seen, involved the only instance of physical violence by an adult on a child in the film, when the mother slapped Mikaël/Laure's face and sent them to their room. Although we later see

Mikaël/Laure and their father sitting on the bed together, in line with Sciamma's child-height approach, we do not get a later scene involving, for example, a late-night, tense, whispered conversation between the parents, trying to figure out together how best to understand what has happened or arguing from opposing positions. In fact, we do not see the parents again at all that evening. Instead, as I have already mentioned, the film cuts to Mikaël/Laure lying in bed the same night but not asleep and being joined in bed by Jeanne. There is no surprise that Jeanne should have come to Mikaël/Laure's room, no attempt to convince her to return to her own bed, but rather a practiced gesture of making space for her in the bed. The familiarity is further emphasized by the whispered conversation that follows. Apparently unrelated to anything that has happened that evening, Jeanne says: "I've got one for you" (j'en ai un pour toi). While the viewer may be momentarily disconcerted and wonder what the "one" refers to, Mikaël/Laure doesn't miss a beat and begins to guess what their sister is thinking of in a game of Who Am I?

There is, of course, nothing anodyne in the choice of game here and in its explicit focus on questions of identity and the clues that reveal that identity. It also serves to remind us, though, of the utter randomness of childhood exchanges. For the adult viewer, the events of the evening are upsetting, concerning, and troubling, and they have clearly triggered similar feelings in the two children. Mikaël/Laure is lying awake in bed and Jeanne has obviously been unable or unwilling to sleep in her own bed. However, the children do not explicitly acknowledge this. Instead, what we see and hear is the kind of momentary lapse into the absurd to which Who Am I? often gives rise, couched in the kind of familiarity that we recognize in games siblings play:

JEANNE: I've got one.
MIKAËL/LAURE: Is it a woman?
J: No.
M/L: A man?
J: Yes.

M/L: Is it someone we know in real life?
J: No.
M/L: Is he on TV?
J: Yes.
M/L: Do we like him?
J: Not really.
M/L: Is he handsome?
J [seems to consider her response]: No.
M/L: Does he have hair?
J: No.
M/L: Is he in a programme?
J: Em, no.
M/L: I know! Is he in an advert? It's the fat guy from the pasta advert!

As well as the combination of absurdity and familiarity, what we are also struck by here, of course, is the binary gender opposition in Mikaël/Laure's opening two questions (Is it a woman? Is it a man?) and the focus on aspects of physical appearance as determinants of identity through almost all the other questions. On one level, this represents a moment of unspoken solidarity between siblings. However, coming after the complete breakdown of the division between Mikaël-outdoors and Laure-indoors, it is also an opportunity for Sciamma to remind us of the complexities of Mikaël/Laure's strategies for navigating their identity *and* the simultaneously simplistic assumptions of gender binaries that both children apparently hold.

The focus remains on the bedroom and the morning light comes through the window onto the bed, signalling the arrival of a new day. The mother enters the room – one of only two occasions we see her doing this in the whole film – and gently wakens Jeanne, quietly asking her to return to her own bed. Jeanne leaves, and when the mother shakes Mikaël/Laure to wake them up, she says that they need to get dressed. Mikaël/Laure sleepily starts to pull on shorts while asking what they are going to do. Their mother tells them they are going to their friends' houses to "explain" what happened. She also insists that Mikaël/Laure must wear a dress, handing them a blue T-shirt dress to pull on despite the child's obvious resistance and fear. The latter makes for uncomfortable viewing, all the more so because the scene unfolds in a space that we know Mikaël/Laure has considered safe for them. Indeed, it is worth noting that in a joint interview of Sciamma and French author Annie Ernaux, published in the French feminist magazine *La Déferlante*, the latter describes this scene as "awful" insofar as it plunges the viewer into the heart of "the tragedy of childhood." Sciamma responds by stating that were she making the film today, she would not shoot this scene again: "I wouldn't be able to film such violence" (Sciamma and Ernaux, 2021, 8). While Sciamma does not explicitly state why she decided to include the scene in the first place, she notes that it was often rejected by audiences after screenings of the film because "people can't stand to see adult domination over children being represented, despite the fact that it is everywhere" (2021, 8–9). In other words, there is an implicit assertion that audiences refuse to see, and thus to acknowledge, what Sciamma goes on to describe as "THE great scandal" (LE grand scandale), namely "a naturalised domination" (2021, 9).

To return to the significance of the bedroom as a locus of childhood, within a few onscreen minutes, Mikaël/Laure's room has alternately served as: a space to which they are banished after an act of violence; a site of almost non-verbal exchange with their father; a quiet place where they can reflect on what has happened; a space where trust between siblings can be demonstrated; a backdrop to the apparent absurdity of a childish game of Who Am I?; and finally a context in which the violence of "adult domination over children" figures once more. Despite the brief intrusions of grown-up violence or its aftermath, earlier scenes had already served, in small, everyday ways, to underscore the comparative safety of this specific space for Mikaël/Laure, even when adults appear. This is perhaps most notably the case in a scene that is rarely discussed, after Mikaël/Laure's first encounter with the other children. When Mikaël/

Figure 22
Mikaël/Laure in homemade swimming trunks.

Laure returns home, they reveal to their mother that they have left the apartment without telling her. The mother scolds them gently, since, after all, Mikaël/Laure is a ten-year-old child who has just arrived in a new town and presumably has not yet found their way about. However, a short while after, as Mikaël/Laure unpacks boxes of comics onto the shelves of their bedroom, the mother comes to see them with a gift and, importantly, a token of trust in the shape of an apartment key that she has tied onto a pink shoestring. When the mother leaves the room, Mikaël/Laure switches the pink shoestring for a less gendered white shoelace from their trainer and hangs it happily around their neck.

The bedroom setting also serves as a backdrop to Mikaël/Laure's trimming down of their red, all-in-one swimsuit to transform it into a pair of trunks that will enable them to accompany the other children on a swimming trip to the lake. However, the hastily cobbled-together trunks alone are not sufficient from Mikaël/Laure's perspective. I will discuss, in the next chapter, their fabrication of a Play-Doh penis. But what is significant, in relation to the discussion of the bedroom here, is that Mikaël/Laure checks their appearance and the physical transformation brought about when they put the Play-Doh penis in their trunks in the mirror on the inside of their wardrobe door. In other words, for Mikaël/Laure, the bedroom is a safe space. It is a space where they can adapt the details of their appearance and presentation of self so that they have the confidence to continue passing as Mikaël, apparently unconcerned that they will be interrupted by a parent or sibling.

With all that in mind, the intrusion of the mother the morning after seems doubly violent and cruel in its impact on that safe space. The film establishes a clear division between the indoor, domestic sphere (where the central child figure is, at least initially, only "Laure") and the outdoor, public world of childhood games, the friendship group, the forest, and the lake (where the child is, until the very last frames of the film, "Mikaël"). When movement goes from domestic to external, from indoor to outdoor, from private to public, there is no threat as such. Indeed, with the crucial exception of their mother making them leave the apartment to tell their friends that they are "Laure," movement from indoors to outdoors, whether undertaken alone or in the company of another child, is always voluntary, always consensual. From the very first foray outdoors alone when they meet Lisa, Mikaël/Laure's movement from the private to the public sphere is always of their own volition and often follows a new step in what we can read as their attempts at passing, whether consciously or not: observing their torso in the bathroom mirror then joining in with the football bare-chested or checking the shape of the bulge in their swimming trunks created by the Play-Doh penis.

However, the film's turning points tend to come when the movement is reversed – when the outdoor world encroaches on the domestic. Such intrusions are signalled each time by the doorbell, a domestic harbinger of trouble for

Mikaël/Laure with a banality that underlines the irony of the everyday being able to disrupt and, indeed, *inter*rupt their life in such a temporarily catastrophic way. It happens first when Lisa comes to the door early in the film, while Jeanne is drawing Mikaël/Laure's portrait. After an exchange with Lisa whispered through the thick front door, they extricate themselves from the sitting. It happens again when Jeanne has been left at home alone, and Lisa rings the doorbell, looking for Mikaël, with a ripple effect that extends to the latter's return from the shopping trip with their mother and the deal brokered with Jeanne to win her silence. And then it happens again when Rayan and his mother ring the doorbell and Mikaël/Laure's mother learns that they are Mikaël for the other children. On each occasion, the doorbell interrupts a quiet household, emphasizing the extent to which "the true menace to Laure's identity comes from outside" (English 2019, 43). In this final example, when Rayan and his mother appear at the door, the glances exchanged by the siblings indoors clearly suggest that the sound marks a break from their routine, from what is predictable in their existence. And, of course, the mother's insistence that Mikaël/Laure should go to Rayan and Lisa's homes with her, that they should be the ones outside the doors ringing the bells, brings further disruption to the delicate equilibrium that had been established.

Children at Play

Backdrops are significant in and of themselves: we make sense of the lives of the characters in *Tomboy* not only through our reading of those backdrops but also, of course, via the activities that play out against them. The settings Sciamma uses, whether indoors or outdoors, are helpful in terms of what they convey about the dynamic between the family members, in the division they enable Sciamma to construct between public and private, and in what they offer the children by way of spaces to explore the world around them and their relationship with it and with each other. However, it is also crucial to consider what we see of the children's lives and how Sciamma goes about filming the games, conversations, and silences of the children's everyday.

Partly because the film is set during the school holidays and focuses on children who are spending their holidays at home, rather than attending summer camp or a similar structure, and partly because of Sciamma's overt decision to film at child height, it is unsurprising that play should be a common focus of the children's daily routines. I would suggest, though, that the very extent to which we watch the children playing games or engaging in other forms of creative play is striking, constituting a succession of choreographies of childhood. I have already mentioned some examples in previous sections and will discuss others in more detail below, but, by way of a non-exhaustive list and in no particular order, we have football, Happy Families, Who Am I?, water-bottle fighting, play wrestling, hide and seek, Play-Doh sculpting, Truth or Dare, a short and tutu-clad dance routine with improvised accompaniment on the Bontempi organ, scenarios acted out using bath toys and showerheads transformed into microphones, the application of makeup in order to "dress up as girls," and some kind of competitive team game I confess to not wholly understanding involving individuals being called upon from opposing teams to try and be the first to grab a sweatshirt lying equidistant between the teams, possibly a variation on Capture the Flag … that seems like a lot of playing to fit into a film that is only eighty-two minutes in length.

Some of the games and play activities involve children on their own, others occur with two children playing together (more often than not, Mikaël/Laure and Jeanne), and others still involve the wider friendship group. While examples of the first two categories crop up across the discussion in this book as they contribute to an examination of, for example, the film's exploration of the development of the children's individual identities, I turn primarily to the third category now, to consider what happens when Sciamma films her cast of children playing together.

The first thing to note is that none of these scenes take place indoors. They are all outdoor activities, the significance of which primarily comes in terms of the public/private division I have already discussed. But outdoor activities also place the children away from the watchful gaze of parents and carers. The children choose their outdoor games, set their own rules, and decide who can or cannot participate. There is no interruption in the shape of a parent calling someone back in for mealtime or a random adult figure instructing them not to play in a particular place or in a specific way. The universe they inhabit while playing together as a group is an adult-free zone in which the children learn how to interact with other children, albeit through "forms of engagement [... that] conform to norms that participants seem intuitively to understand" (Smith 2023b, 147). Speaking in 2012, Sciamma noted that sport featured in her first two films (*Naissance des pieuvres* and *Tomboy*) because it offered her an opportunity to explore what it means to be part of a group, the question of integration within a group. In her words: "A group is always a bit like a team playing together" (cited in Vallet 2012). Although Sciamma's comments here relate to her first films, it is worth noting that sport also features in *Bande de filles*, in fact, via its rather incongruous opening sequence, which shows an American football game. This is the first thing we see, before we are introduced to any characters or to the geographical or temporal setting of the film: two teams in American football gear, wearing helmets, and playing on a floodlit pitch. As the sequence and the game end, we discover that the players are women, something that is rather destabilizing, first because audiences do not draw an immediate connection between American football and contemporary France and, second, because American football, at least in the French and broader European context, remains a sport we assume is predominantly played by men.

While *Tomboy* does not present sports in the same institutionally structured way as *Naissance des pieuvres* with its depiction of the world of competitive synchronized swimming, the two scenes where the children play football

Figure 23
Watching football.

together clearly contribute to our understanding of their group dynamic and, in particular, our understanding of processes of inclusion and exclusion, whether self-imposed or a product of group decisions and actions.

The scenes occur within the first half hour of the film and, as such, play a key role in establishing Mikaël/Laure's relationship with the other children in the group, as well as with Lisa and with their own body. In the first scene, which comes around the twenty-minute mark, Mikaël/Laure and Lisa are on the sidelines of the concrete football pitch and Mikaël/Laure seems to be paying close attention to the other kids as they play. The camera stays tightly focused on small groups as the children run in and out of the shot. We see them shooting for a goal, congratulating each other, racing after the ball, briefly bursting into a snippet of football stadium favourite "Seven Nation Army" by the White Stripes, and so on.

Some of the children are playing bare-chested, some spit on the ground as they run, and the camera focuses on Mikaël/Laure's face as they follow the action, partly just watching the game in progress but also, it becomes clear from a couple of shot–reverse shots, concentrating on the gestures and movements of individual children. Through a brief exchange between Mikaël/Laure and Lisa, it becomes apparent that Lisa's status as spectator, rather than participant, is not voluntary but a product of the other (male) children's decision that she is "nulle" ("bad" or "poor") where football is concerned. Lisa continues to observe Mikaël/Laure watching the game, a triangulation of gazes. When Mikaël/Laure realizes that they are also an object of scrutiny, they ask Lisa what she is looking at, to which she responds that Mikaël/Laure is "not like the others." As Darren Waldron observes, while such scenes foreground Mikaël/Laure's engagement with their own performance of gender, they also "reveal the conditionality of all gendering by highlighting the performative strategies undertaken by boys to comply with compulsory masculinity" (2013, 60), as the film "posits an understanding of gender that is at once 'authentic' and 'put on'" (Lindner 2018, 201).

The precise time that elapses between different scenes is often difficult to chart in the film. There are no explicit references to something happening "the next day" or "two weeks later," either through dialogue or, for example, onscreen captions. However, the first football scene is separated from the second by three sequences that take place chronologically in the evening of the same day and then on the following morning. The first of these sees the family together in the living room, each engaged in their own activity but sharing the communal space. The first of the longer sequences in which we watch Mikaël/Laure considering their own body in the bathroom mirror follows. The lighting and activities suggest that the third scene takes place the following day and gives us the opportunity to admire Jeanne's tutu-clad dance routine with Mikaël/Laure's plonking Bontempi accompaniment. The action then cuts to a shot of the same concrete football pitch, with the blue-grey wall against which Mikaël/Laure had been standing during the first game, and we watch them arrive from a little pathway through trees behind the wall.

They once again position themselves in front of the wall, standing out visually due to the red flash of their shorts and framed alone in the centre of the image as the young footballers all chase away after the ball to the left. Mikaël/Laure stays on the margins until the boys trot back into frame and the game resumes; this time they ask if they can join, and are given permission to become part of one of the teams. Since Lisa has previously told Mikaël/Laure that the others refuse to let her play football with them, there is clearly an initial indication of group acceptance in their invitation to "Mikaël" and one that we, as viewers, assume stems from their gendering of Mikaël as a boy and Lisa as a girl.

The banality of this act of "passing" is telling. The camera does not close in on Mikaël/Laure's face to offer a glimpse of satisfaction, relief, or pleasure. Rather, we watch a few seconds of the kids playing, skidding on the dusty ground, aiming for a goal, tackling each other, and then we become aware that Mikaël/Laure is carefully observing the others again, apparently weighing up options. What is going on in their head becomes clear when they take off their T-shirt and continue to play bare-chested like some of the others, briefly looking down at their own torso before resuming the running about, stopping to spit determinedly on the ground. We spot Lisa at the edge of the pitch, and she calls over to "Mikaël," offering her new friend a drink from the plastic bottle of green liquid she is holding (mint syrup, we assume, given the bright flash of colour), and complimenting them on their playing abilities.

Over the course of the two scenes, particularly because they come in such quick succession, we get a glimpse of the differing layers of integration and processes of inclusion and exclusion playing out simultaneously. The newcomer is allowed to watch but not initially invited to join the game, partly, we assume, because they are identified as being friends with Lisa. When the same newcomer turns up alone, they are invited to play with the others, and it is once again Lisa whose peripheral status is foregrounded. When she appears, watching from the sidelines, she explicitly calls Mikaël over rather than attempting to engage with the rest of the group. There are, very obviously, codes, conventions, and habits to be navigated here, and Lisa has come to understand that there are situations where she will be considered an outsider to the group. These codes, conventions, and habits become all the more important when you know – as we do explicitly by the second football scene – that Mikaël is also Laure and that they are not only keen to become part of the game but also to be able to integrate into the group as Mikaël. At one and the same time, Sciamma depicts the group's potential to include and exclude, as well as demonstrating the mundane ways in which children seem to adjust to the group. And we are left in a complicated position.

The same set of stereotypical views of gender that mean Lisa is excluded from the football games but allowed to play with the others in all other contexts also form the basis of the gestures and actions Mikaël/Laure seeks to capture in their desire to be invited to join one of the teams. We find ourselves rooting for the central child in their attempts to pass in ways that are dependent on a particular and traditionally binary vision of gendered performance – largely out of concern and fear for what a "discovery" might trigger. And yet, at the same time, we feel frustrated that Lisa is excluded from specific games on the basis of her gender and male expectations of her gender.

We will return to another group play scene in the discussion of textures, surfaces, and materiality in the next chapter but, for the moment, I want to focus on the depiction of a similar physical exuberance and joy earlier in the film when Mikaël/Laure goes to Lisa's house to play. The pair are in Lisa's bedroom. She puts on music and starts to dance, pulling at an initially reluctant Mikaël/Laure's arms to encourage them to join her. The resistance is short-lived and soon both children are bopping around, grinning wildly, limbs flailing to the delightful pop rhythms of Para One's music. Both Lisa and Mikaël/Laure are absorbed in enjoying the physicality of dance and the movement of their own bodies. This may be a good point for me to come out as a *non*-dancer, so this lack of inhibitions is somewhat incomprehensible to me

– but, in some ways, it is that very incomprehensibility that makes the joy of the children even easier to read. There is nothing but music (the only instance of diegetic music) and movement and, when the music stops, two exhausted, happy children. Furthermore, as I will set out in more detail in the next chapter, the bedroom dancing scene's combination of sheer sensory physicality – with its emphasis on surfaces and textures through the application of make-up – not only provides a key example of the ways in which Sciamma takes Lisa's bedroom seriously as a locus of childhood but also serves as a clear indication of the importance she places on childhood as lived through the senses, through textures, and through children's embodied experiences.

Alongside a general tendency towards the ludic subversion of conventionally adult-centred spaces, as we have seen, Sciamma's narrative plays out – pun absolutely intended – against a series of backdrops in which children are left to their own devices. These are spaces where they decide on the rules of inclusion and exclusion, spaces that lend themselves as much to the dynamic movement and action of childhood as to its moments of more quiet contemplation. This absolutely does not mean that *Tomboy*'s childscapes are uncomplicatedly positive, utopian spaces where children roam free and play happily, away from the gaze of adults who, in the context of other, more conventional cinematic narratives of childhood, might be overprotective or, indeed, threatening. Rather, it means that Sciamma takes seriously the loci of childhood as sites of significant interactions between individuals and between those individuals and their environment. Those individuals just happen to be children. Their interactions are significant both in the sense that we understand them as playing a role in the development of the children themselves but also, of course, as reflections of pre-existing social codes and norms.

Chapter 3

Textures, Surfaces, and Materiality: The Stuff of Childhood

In the previous chapters, we have seen how *Tomboy* sits within Sciamma's oeuvre to date, how it builds on some of the tropes that were already evident in *Naissance des pieuvres*, and how it paves the way not only for *Bande de filles*, the third film in her loose "coming of age trilogy," but also for the hugely successful *Portrait de la jeune fille en feu* and for *Petite Maman*. I have examined Sciamma's use of the loci of childhood, from football pitches to bedrooms – these spaces that she takes seriously as sites of meaningful interaction between children, of individual identity development, and of the complicated navigation of the codes and conventions of childhood. I have explored the activities we watch the children engage in against these backdrops, focusing particularly on how the choreography of games and creative play structure their experiences. Across these discussions, the emphasis has been on the ways that Sciamma keeps the film at child height, offering Mikaël/Laure a space within which to explore ways of being in the world, centring on what they *do* rather than raising the question of *why* they might act or behave in certain ways. As I have argued, this approach, this desire not to psychologize the "gender non-conformist child" (Waldron 2013, 60), and not to offer up space for discussion of possible motivation, is fundamental to the film's queerness.

In this final chapter, I argue that there is one further facet of Sciamma's filmmaking, present across her output and already obvious in *Tomboy*, that opens a path for her not only to depict the complexities of a queer "coming into desire" (Bradbury-Rance 2019, 85) but to cover new ground in the queering of childhood subjectivities onscreen. I am thinking here of her distinctive and deliberate use of textures, surfaces, and materiality that further embed the film within a contemporary vision of what queer cinemas are and what they can be, queering the very stuff of cinematic childhood.

That this is a film of textures and materiality, and people's – in particular, children's – experience thereof, is evident from the opening images. I have described how we are introduced to the figure who will turn out to be its central character, Mikaël/Laure, as they are travelling in a car with their father through the quiet streets of an anonymous suburb. I have examined the ways in which the fact that the child is being allowed to drive the car, sitting on their father's knee, positions us at child height from *Tomboy*'s earliest moments, and I suggest that, read alongside shots of the child's legs dangling from a balcony or the unpredictability of the geometry of children's games in a later water fight, these opening images also introduce us to a child who is at an oblique angle to the world around them. What I further argue here, though, is that this occurs not only through the interaction between child and adult or between child and new activity but also through the interaction between that child and the world around them, as "the gender nonconformist child [becomes] an embodied subject defined by her relations to the outside world" (Waldron 2013, 64). This interaction is partly mediated via the car, the steering wheel, and the child's questions about turning and how to switch on the indicator. However, before the child is even remotely "anchored" physically, it is also an immediate interaction between child and world, child and air, child and light.

And we can understand the uses to which Sciamma puts such bodily, sensory, and corporeal realities and experiences all the more clearly if we consider the recent turn towards phenomenological approaches in film studies and the productive dialogues that have emerged through the intersection of phenomenologically inspired film studies, in its turn, with feminist and queer studies. After all, "phenomenology can offer a resource for queer studies insofar as it emphasizes the importance of lived experience, the intentionality of consciousness, the significance of nearness or what is ready-to-hand, and the role of repeated and habitual actions in shaping bodies and worlds" (Ahmed 2006, 2). *Tomboy* shows profound "haptic visuality," as Laura Marks defines it – namely it is a film that "privileges the material presence of the image," often "connect[ing] directly to sense perception" and "encourag[ing] a bodily relationship between the viewer and the image" (2000, 163–4). As Katharina Lindner notes, such "foregrounding of queer modes of embodiment, movement and spatiality are key to the 'queerness' of Sciamma's queer feminist cinema" (2018, 143).

Encounters between Body and World

The film opens on blurry images of leaves dappled by sunlight and a sound we are not immediately able to recognize, but which we quickly realize is air rushing past and the sound of tires on a road, "gradually discovering what is in the image rather than coming to the image already knowing what it is" (Marks 2000, 178). The camera pans slowly downwards until the back of a head fills the centre of the frame, a child's head, we assume, given its size and the thickness of the neck. The head is covered in dark blonde hair, shaggy, moving in the breeze; we catch glimpses of wisps of thin hair on the nape of the neck in the light. We can also see the top of a blue crewneck T-shirt, and the focus is tight enough for us to be able to see the grain of the cloth. As well as the close-up of the back of the child's head, neck, and shoulders, we also see a close-up of their hand, framed from halfway up their forearm, so detached and disembodied but immersed in the air and the light. Before we see the child's face, before we learn anything about them, before we discover how they come to be moving through the world in this way, at this speed, at this odd angle to their surroundings, we meet them as a sensory being. We hear the same rush of air that whooshes past them, we see the tufts of their hair ruffle in the breeze, and we watch their hand twist around in the air.[1]

Their presence as a sensory being is not exclusively a product of their interactions with the public spaces of the outside world, nor of that world's interactions with them. Rather, it continues across those opening minutes of the film, after the brief car journey, as the child enters the private sphere and wanders around their new apartment, continuing to develop "a relationship with the world that is at once a mutual and intimate relation of contact" (Barker 2009, 3). The rooms themselves are relatively nondescript and will only really come alive as the family begins to inhabit them. However, even in these earlier stages, we understand that it is Mikaël/Laure's physical interaction with their surroundings that is important, not least because the camera lingers on their hands as they run over the surfaces of walls and doorways on their way through the apartment. Or rather, Mikaël/Laure's hands linger in the frame. Sciamma makes use of rather static framing in these interior shots, creating a space through which the protagonist can move instead of following them or offering us a more conventional view of their new surroundings. The film opened with a foregrounding of Mikaël/Laure's embodied experience of the world around them. Here, again, indoors, it is a physical embodiment, a tactile and sensory encounter with the surroundings that we also experience as Mikaël/Laure takes stock of their new home. They quite literally feel their way around the rooms, as though to emphasize that their presence here will be a lived and sensory experience. Sciamma is offering us another example of what Jennifer Barker has described as touch that signifies "not simply contact, but rather a profound manner of being, a mode through which the body … presents and expresses itself to the world and through which it perceives that same world as sensible" (2009, 2).

Against this backdrop, my goal in this final chapter is twofold. On the one hand, I am fascinated by the textures, surfaces, and materials of childhood that make up the lives of Mikaël/Laure and the other children, in and of themselves, from tree bark and the snap of branches in the forest to urine and saliva via Play-Doh, chewing gum, and soapy bath suds. On the other hand, I am also clear that we make sense of these textures, surfaces, and materials through the children's interactions with them. On occasion, those interactions are conscious, and we are sometimes witness to a deliberate consideration, whether through a verbal exchange or by the camera focusing on an expression of pleasure, satisfaction, or disgust, for example. However, at times the interactions are presented in a less mediated fashion. They are physical, bodily, sensory, and we simply observe the children engaging with their lived environment, carving out a place for their bodies within it, without the film slowing down to show us their reactions or responses. In the introduction to their edited volume on *Childhood and Nation in Contemporary World Cinema*, Stephanie Hemelryk Donald, Emma Wilson, and Sarah Wright note that "emotional impact and identification are (arguably, of course) sharper on screen when there is a child protagonist in play, whether because we *take responsibility for the child* or because we *project our own remembered childishness onto the protagonist*" (2018, 3, my emphasis). This is doubtless true but, in relation to *Tomboy* and its use of the textures and materiality of childhood, I am also interested in those elements that are not mediated through reason or through the prism of adult reflection but that rather stay within the child-height realm of Sciamma's film. After all, as Emma Wilson has observed, "what Sciamma avoids as far as possible … is the construction of a child by an adult looking back. The inscrutability of her children is a part of her acknowledgement of their autonomy" (2021, 45). I have written elsewhere (Johnston 2021) about the circulation of objects in Sciamma's work, the significance of those objects (from apple cores to books), and the significance of the very act of circulation. Here, though, I am not interested in the objects themselves, as such, but rather in their textures, surfaces, and materiality, that which "tends" towards the children, and the ways in which "bodies and their objects tend toward each other … are orientated toward each other, and are shaped by this orientation" (Ahmed 2006, 51).

Swimming Trunks and Play-Doh Penises

By way of an initial example, we can take the Play-Doh scene I have referred to in passing in previous chapters. It can, of course, be read as tremendously important for what it tells us about Mikaël/Laure's relationship with their body and the concerns they have about the visibility of their body in the public sphere. We have already watched as they examined their own chest, shoulders, and arms, partly in order to compare their own torso to those of the children who played football with their shirts off, but also to assess whether that was something they, too, might be able to do and to be able to "pass" in doing, their skin "function[ing] … as both a covering and an uncovering" (Barker 2009, 28). When Lisa announces that the kids are going swimming the next day, though, it triggers a different set of concerns and anxieties because Mikaël/Laure needs to think about the shape and style of their bathing suit since they have a body we would typically gender as female, not male. Specifically, there is no bulge from a pre-pubescent penis in the DIY swimming trunks – and this, we quickly discover, is the situation Mikaël/Laure seeks to remedy. We do not know whether this stems from a concern about not passing, a desire to see their body as they expect to see that of the boys in the group, or some combination of concern and desire. There is no internal monologue and certainly no external dialogue, nobody with whom Mikaël/Laure can talk this through. What we do understand, though, is that the swimming trip preparations are not completed by simply trimming down a bathing suit. And that is where the Play-Doh comes in …

Mikaël/Laure makes the sartorial adjustments to the swimming costume in their bedroom, away from the prying gaze of the rest of the family. However, rather than staying there for what comes next, the action cuts to the kitchen, a much lighter, brighter, and, importantly, *communal* room. The kitchen table is centre-frame, and Jeanne sits at the table, working on a jigsaw puzzle. Mikaël/Laure appears – another instance of a static camera, an immobile frame, and what happens just having to fit within that frame. They have a box

Figure 24
The Play-Doh sequence.

in their arms, overflowing with brightly coloured plastic bits and pieces, and, in a small but nonetheless significant act of spatial appropriation, they place the box on the already cluttered table, sliding Jeanne's jigsaw over to make room for what they have to do. Jeanne asks a couple of times precisely what Mikaël/Laure is making, but they refuse to respond. Mikaël/Laure takes a chunk of Play-Doh, rolls it into a small cylinder, gauges the appropriateness of its dimensions, and rolls it some more until they are finally satisfied with their creation.

There are two aspects of this scene that I find particularly interesting. First, I find it striking that it is something that happens "in plain sight." There is no hiding away, no taking advantage of being alone in a room – as occurs, for instance, when Mikaël/Laure checks their body in the bathroom mirror. Quite the opposite. Mikaël/Laure makes a deliberate decision to make the Play-Doh penis while sitting at the table in a shared family space and next to Jeanne.

Mikaël/Laure walks a tightrope between, on the one hand, a refusal to talk about what they are doing, to name what they are making, and, on the other, the openness of the act of creation. Second, what I find surprising about the sequence is that the focus is not solely on Mikaël/Laure's Play-Doh creation but, instead, alongside the rather more practical moulding of the penis we also see Jeanne leave her jigsaw puzzle to one side and begin to play with the Play-Doh. Specifically, she wants to make Play-Doh spaghetti and needs Mikaël/Laure's assistance in putting together a contraption that will allow her to get the right fitting to turn her lump of Play-Doh into coloured strands. And what is most striking, from my perspective at least, is the joy that comes across as the siblings play together, "allied and complicit" (Wilson 2021, 53). Mikaël/Laure is definitely focused on the task at hand, but they still stop to help Jeanne; the pair giggle together at the process, and they take delight in the absurdity of the strands of Play-Doh oozing out. There is a practical purpose and outcome to the scene, and as soon as Mikaël/Laure is happy with the Play-Doh penis, they leave Jeanne to play alone. However, the two also take delight in the physicality of their play and in the peculiar materiality of the substance they are playing with.

I would also argue that, as much as we can interpret the bathing suit and Play-Doh scenes as focusing on transformation, they are also about the layering and un-layering of textures and materials and the multidimensionality of the children's engagement with their environment. As so often happens in *Tomboy* and in Sciamma's other films, we are faced with scenes within scenes, encouraged to focus on a specific, concrete (or in this case, Play-Doh) detail, but then through that same detail invited to recognize the experience of the detail, "the *tactile and tangible* patterns and structures of significance" (Barker 2009, 25) it offers us. We watch as Mikaël/Laure cuts the one-piece bathing suit, but we also listen to the sound of the scissors cutting through the fabric; we watch as the box of plastic is brought through and the Play-Doh mechanisms are pieced together, but we also imagine the feel of the dough in the children's hands and, for anybody who has ever played with the stuff, we rec-

Figure 25
Tomboy: The Play-Doh penis.

ollect its pasty smell and the simultaneous grain and grease of its surface; our "memory … [is] encoded in touch, sound, perhaps smell, more than in vision" (Marks 2000, 129).

The swimming scene itself is also significant insofar as it offers a further opportunity to observe the group of children in a new context, playing different games, and, crucially, displaying their bodies in a different way. Just as the small concrete football pitch had offered a frame that sometimes contained the children but beyond which they also ran, jumped, and slid, as we saw in the previous chapter, so too does Sciamma's camerawork in the swimming scenes impose a frame, insofar as the children's games centre on and around a small platform floating in the lake. It is hard to estimate its size, but it is big enough to hold half a dozen young children at any one time, offers a point of departure for leaps into the water, and serves as a rather unstable surface on which the children play-wrestle with the aim of pushing their opponent into the lake. Once again, the children are alone and not under adult supervision in this short scene, and once again, they choose their games and the rules of their games – but what is particularly noteworthy is the focus on their bodies and on those bodies as sites of experience.

In many ways, the football scenes analyzed in the previous chapter lend themselves particularly well to a consideration of rules and conventions in children's games. This is partly because football depends on players playing by the same set of rules. However, it also comes with a further layer of conventions operating at the level of the children's engagement with gender. The build-up to the swimming scene certainly reminds us of those gender codes, but the scene itself is unmoored from more land-bound practices and behaviours. The children can throw themselves into the air and let themselves divebomb into the water, they can slide about on the surface of the little platform and slip or push others into the lake, they can stand upright gazing at the sun, or they can crouch down and shiver with goosebumps on their skin. Their bodies are theirs to do with as they will, and we are reminded that "skin connects as well as contains" (Ahmed 2006, 54) or, as Jennifer Barker puts it, that skin represents "a place of constant contact between the outside and the inside" (2009, 28). For Mikaël/Laure, there are still risks that come with this apparent freedom and with the risk they take in physically sharing space with the other children in this way. They are obviously concerned about whether they will continue to pass or not, but they also join in the games with the other children, including playfully wrestling on the edge of the floating platform with one of their friends. We might contrast this relationship to the body with what we see in the synchronized swimming sequences in *Naissance des pieuvres*. There, above water, the swimmers are poise and order personified, counting out the beat that governs their every move in a "performance of femininity." Under the surface of the water, though, we see the chaos of legs, arms, and bodies, "a monstrous, allegorical body" (Chevalier 2019, 69) and the streams of bubbles their movement creates, crisscrossing the screen: "The

Figure 26
Synchronized swimming in *Naissance des pieuvres.*

perfect façade of the girls above water … contrasts with the struggle and effort each girl makes beneath its surface" (Jonet 2017, 1132).[2]

By contrast, what is striking in the swimming scene in *Tomboy* is the extent to which the children just seem to become bodies experiencing the world in all its textures, surfaces, and materiality, something we see again in another group scene when the children have a play water fight. Then, too, it is a hot and sunny day, and the core group of children have gone out together to play. The scene happens after Jeanne has learned that her sibling is passing as Mikaël with their new friends, so Jeanne is also there, along with a wider group of children we haven't previously seen. There are some smaller-scale encounters and conversations between small clusters of children, but there is also a sudden explosion of noise and laughter and movement and a blur of bodies onscreen when the water battle erupts. We are not witness to a buildup to the water fight; rather, there is suddenly shrieking and rapid movement in unpredictable directions, and it takes the viewer a few seconds to make out the details of the scene and understand what is happening. First, there just seems to be chaotic movement, "the crazy energy of childhood" (Wilson 2021, 44), but then we notice arms and hands and clear plastic bottles, and we realize that the flashes darting across the screen, these queer trajectories of childhood are, alternately, jets of water being squeezed out of the bottles and the arms of children rushing at their friends to take better aim at them.

Whereas in *Naissance des pieuvres*, the chaos of limbs and bubbles contrasted so sharply with the calm above the surface of the swimming pool, "the unseen spectacle of the athletes' bodies, indefatigably working to stay afloat" (Smith 2023, 142), in *Tomboy* the chaos is just a joyous, loud, anarchic mess of children enjoying themselves. I describe this chaotic action as a series of "queer trajectories" not because all the children who are involved in this exuberant game are queer but precisely because "Sciamma's vision shows children … as ardent subjects, some queer, some not, all impressionable, aching, changing" (Wilson 2021, 53). As we watch Mikaël/Laure being merrily drenched, we realize the extent to which there is sheer delight for *all* the children involved in the uncomplicated inclusion and sense of belonging to the group.

The blue dress that Mikaël/Laure's mother forces them to wear to "reveal" themselves as "Laure" to Rayan and Lisa and their respective parents conveys a similar, though significantly less joyous, multi-layered experience of textures, surfaces, and materiality. I will return to the materiality, textures, and surfaces of the dress and all they evoke below, but first, I would like to consider its colour. The traditionally masculine blue tone underlines the irony of the dress not being sufficient, in and of itself, to transform the child's presentation of self into that of a "gender-conforming" girl. As I noted earlier, when the family was settling into their new apartment, Mikaël/Laure's mother asked if they liked their new room and specifically commented on the shade of blue of its walls, remarking that it was what Mikaël/Laure had wanted. And as Darren

Figure 27
The water fight.

Waldron has observed, the same blue of Mikaël/Laure's bedroom is replicated in the "grey blue of the wall at the side of the football pitch … characterising public and intimate zones as masculine" (2013, 66). In the previous chapter, I briefly discussed the moment when Mikaël/Laure swaps the apartment-key pink shoestring for a more neutral white shoestring. In fact, the stereotypical contrast between blues and pinks is marked from the opening title sequence of the film: the title flashes up on the screen, and the typeface alternates between a bright blue and a deep reddish pink until it finally lands on a red and blue pattern.

Pink and blue are also used together in a short but nonetheless significant scene when Jeanne draws Mikaël/Laure's portrait. In an image so striking that it was used as the film's poster, we see a seated Mikaël/Laure, framed from the waist up, sitting in front of a wall covered in vertically striped pink and blue wallpaper, with a rather sullen expression. As we quickly learn, their younger sister has imposed this moment of stasis. What I find interesting in this scene, as well as the deliberate choice of the combined blue and pink backdrop, is that Mikaël/Laure has no control over the image that Jeanne is creating. These are not the equal collaborative partners we will see in *Portrait* almost a decade later; instead, the sitter's image is subject to the whims of the artist. Jeanne announces in no uncertain terms that she is giving Mikaël/Laure brown eyes, not blue, and that she is also giving them freckles – "*lots* of freckles," a statement emphasized by the sound of the stubby nib of a felt-tip pen thudding down across a rather large round face on the sheet of white paper in front of Jeanne. The artificiality of gendered divisions in the background and an image of self in the hands not of the individual themselves but of a determined six-year-old in the foreground. This is a clear indication, I would say, that Mikaël/Laure's presentation of self must necessarily, at some point, navigate the social codes of two genders. This is partly represented through the conventions and stereotypes of colour coding, as well as by the more immediate conceptions of identity other people impose and assume.

In my introductory discussion of the critical reception of *Tomboy*, I included a quote from one reviewer (Frois 2011) who referred to the film's use of pink and blue with all the connotations of stereotyped visions of binary gender divisions that those colours imply. This may seem rather unexpected or incongruous in the discussion of a film that apparently goes to great lengths to not rely on gendered binaries and to imply that to understand *this* particular story of a queer childhood, they are not helpful as a framing device. And yet, I would argue, we can see Sciamma's use of the tropes of pink and blue as contributing to the very kind of nuanced discussion she wants to see in cinematic depictions of children or teenagers whose experiences mean that they are often marginalized figures. At no point does Sciamma try to suggest that gender does not exist; or rather, and perhaps more significantly, at no point does she attempt to suggest that the existing codes, conventions, and stereotypes of gender do not have an influence on these children. Instead, Sciamma juxtaposes Mikaël/Laure's engagement with their own body, their new friends, and their new environment alongside moments that actively remind us of the existing codes. The film's temporal setting does allow these few weeks in Mikaël/Laure's life to be depicted as though in something of a bubble, detached from the institutional constraints, for example, that they will have to deal with in the classroom. However, in the meantime, for as long as their life revolves around their family indoors and the new friendship group outdoors and away from any formal institutional structures, there is a bubble within which new possibilities can be explored.[3]

And yet, in a foreshadowing of a similar approach in *Portrait de la jeune fille en feu* where we watch the development of the friendship and then the collaborative creative and sexual relationship between Marianne and Héloïse while having been told, from the film's opening scenes, that their story will end, Sciamma reminds us that those codes and conventions of gender still exist. We understand that it is inevitable that Mikaël/Laure will need to engage with them beyond the timeframe of the summer holidays and, indeed, that they are always already part of the everyday existence of these children. And, in part, this is something Sciamma also chooses to convey through her deliberate use of colour and the stereotypically gendered contrast between blue and pink.

To return to the materiality of the blue dress, though, the first thing to observe is that it is quite literally shoved into the frame by Mikaël/Laure's mother, forcing it into the narrative as she forces it upon her child, "impos[ing] sexed norms … so that s/he remain a girl who does not pass as a boy" (Reeser 2013, 5). The child wears the dress, it is true, they have little choice, but the dress seems detached from their body. It is there, hanging off Mikaël/Laure's bony shoulders, both unfamiliar on this body and defamiliarizing. We can contrast the image of Mikaël/Laure in the blue dress at Rayan's door with, for example, the opening shots of the film and the child in the blue T-shirt seeming to absorb the world around them through their

Figure 28
The blue dress abandoned.

skin, soaking up its light and breeze and sounds. The mournful vertical folds of the blue dress stand in stark contrast to the unpredictability and exuberance of the geometries of childhood that we have watched as they race, splash, and slide across the screen. As Sara Ahmed observes: "The vertical is … normative; it is shaped by the repetition of bodily and social actions over time" (2006, 61). And here the vertical folds stand in contrast to those geometries as much when the dress is hanging off Mikaël/Laure's frame as when they abandon it in the branches of the forest trees.

Dresses are peculiar things across Sciamma's films. This particular blue dress foreshadows another that features in *Bande de filles*; the group of girls steal it during a trip to a shopping mall. That dress features in the film's well-known "Diamonds" sequence – when the central group of friends rent a hotel room and sing along to Rihanna's song "Diamonds," bathed in blue light –

Figure 29
The green dress in *Portrait de la jeune fille en feu.*

and then again, the following day, when Marième/Vic has returned home, and her younger sister sees the dress hanging limply from a full-length mirror. And, of course, moving beyond the "coming of age" trilogy, the glorious green dress in *Portrait of a Lady on Fire* is absolutely central to the film, whether being worn by any of the three women at the heart of the narrative, or rustling as the servant Sophie carries it through the mansion, or in its represented form in the incomplete portrait, or, indeed, in its represented form in the portrait Héloïse does complete. Three dresses in three films, and each time we see the dress being worn and also experience it as fabric, folds, textures, rustling, and so on.

I am reminded of the work of Scottish painter Alison Watt, who recalls being taken to the National Gallery in London as a child and being "drawn to the pictures of fabric and drapery – how it folds, and how it seems to move when the body moves" (cited in Woodward 2016). Since the late 1990s, Watt's work has been taken over by "a complete fascination with fabric … her canvases becoming entirely devoted to expansive, wonderfully detailed studies of swathes, tucks and folds" (Woodward 2016). As Watt herself notes in the same interview: "The surface [of a painting] is incredibly physical … When you're working with [paint], you're not just seeing it, you're feeling it: you're inside its substance." *A Portrait without Likeness*, Watt's 2021 exhibition at the Scottish National Portrait Gallery in Edinburgh, takes this fascination further still. In the exhibition Watt isolated objects (lace handkerchiefs, cabbage leaves, ribbons) from the portraits of eighteenth-century painter Allan Ramsay, whom she had admired for many years – with a particular interest in his paintings of women – and made each the subject of its own portrait, depicted in intricate detail. And, just as in Watt's work we are confronted with the materiality of the object, so too does Sciamma's intimate attention to the objects and details of childhood draw our attention to their surfaces, textures, and materiality, to the way they feel or sound or smell to the characters onscreen – "the substance of cinema touch[ing] us … and leav[ing] a trace on our skins" (Barker 2009, 30). That these objects are there to be experienced is an inescapable observation and constitutive of the queering of childhood we are watching onscreen.

I would also note that it is not only the blue dress in *Tomboy* that offers itself up to this kind of "textural" reading. Rather, we are presented with a veritable collage of fabrics and textures over the course of the film. I find myself wondering whether, just as Sciamma takes the *loci* of childhood seriously in her setting of a scene for this queering of a narration of selfhood, she doesn't also take just as seriously the *costumes* of childhood. After all, across her films, much is made of the typical attire of childhood and adolescence.

In *Naissance des pieuvres*, we might think of the ill-fitting jeans Anne wears while she waddles around the mall or the spangled surface of the swimsuit (a one-piece) that Floriane offers Marie. In *Tomboy*, we have everything from the sweater that lies on the forest floor between the opposing teams of kids the first time Mikaël/Laure plays with the other children to Jeanne's tutu during her improvised dance routine. Or we might think of the hoodie Mikaël/Laure wears on their return from Lisa's house in a vain attempt to hide their made-up face from their mother and, of course, the swimsuit that begins as a bright red one-piece and ends as trunks with their ragged edge folded over to disguise their homemade-ness.

In *Bande de filles*, we might also think of denim again in girls' clothing or of Vic's hoodie. The latter offers a particular visual link, I would suggest, between *Tomboy* and *Bande de filles*, insofar as we see the central characters of both films, shot from behind, walking through the concrete walkways of a housing block, hood up over their head, hands shoved into pockets. The hoodie offers protection from the outside world because it places another layer, a second skin, between the wearer and the environment. This second skin also momentarily masks gender. Considered together, *Tomboy* and *Bande de filles* offer a visual foreshadowing of the first walk Héloïse and Marianne undertake together in *Portrait* when the former is waiting downstairs at the door for the latter to join her, enveloped in a long flowing cape with its hood up. The camera follows Héloïse as she walks out of the house; the hood falls back to reveal her hair as her pace quickens and becomes more determined. There is no masking of gender here, but as the film progresses, Héloïse and Marianne's willingness to show themselves to each other becomes increasingly significant.

To return to *Tomboy*, the hoodie and the way we see Mikaël/Laure framed from behind suggests a multiplicity of trajectories that they might follow. As Sara Ahmed puts it: "Having not turned around, who knows where we might turn. Not turning also affects what we can do" (2006, 107). For Ahmed, such "not turning" opens up possibilities for a new lesbian queer politics insofar as it represents a deliberate decision not to respond: "We hear the hail, and even feel its force on the surface of the skin, but we do not turn around, even when those words are directed toward us" (2006, 107). In *Tomboy*, the outcome is similar. While it's true that nobody calls Mikaël/Laure's name here, Ahmed's words are nevertheless relevant insofar as this is the first moment in the film when they do not present themselves openly to the camera. And we are struck by this apparent attempt to conceal something.

We are all the more struck by it because the last thing we saw happening onscreen was Lisa beginning to put makeup on Mikaël/Laure. In the context of my concluding consideration of surfaces and textures this makes the sequence doubly significant. It comes after the scene where we see the two friends hanging out together in Lisa's bedroom. Most of the scene is taken up by dancing, but when the dancing ends and Mikaël/Laure flops onto a sofa, Lisa sits down next to them and opens a box, the contents of which we do not see. Mikaël/Laure asks what she's going to do, and Lisa explains that she's going to put makeup on them: "On va se déguiser en filles" (we're going to dress up as girls).[4] The linguistic implications of the statement are fascinating insofar as they reveal a specific coding of gender and an implicit recognition, from Lisa, that Mikaël/Laure does not fit within those codes and norms – but also, through the use of the plural, that she, Lisa, does not quite fit them either. However, rather than returning to questions of language here and pondering precisely what Lisa might mean by "en filles," I would like to focus on this as an act that necessarily involves surfaces and textures and, specifically, the skin and body of Mikaël/Laure as a canvas for Lisa's makeup.[5]

What is complicated here, in terms of the dynamic between the two children, is that there isn't really any scope for Mikaël/Laure to refuse to be made up. There is a clear hesitation, and they request Lisa not to do "too much" in a manner that reminds us of a similar instruction to Jeanne during the hair trimming. There is a difference between, on the one hand, the transformations of appearance over which Mikaël/Laure has full control (when they adapt their own swimsuit and create the Play-Doh penis) and transformations where they have relinquished a degree of that control and have placed themselves and their body in the hands of someone else. We do not see the result of the makeup sequence in Lisa's bedroom; there is a cut, and we are in the in-between space of the concrete walkway that takes Mikaël/Laure back towards their own home, their hood firmly pulled up so we can't see their face. The camera watches from inside the apartment as the door opens when they get home; Mikaël/Laure comes in quietly, trying to get to a room where they can wash off the makeup before anyone spots them. The attempt fails and their mother, having heard them coming in, calls through to them. When they go to find their mother, hood still up, she naturally notices the makeup, and we see, for the first time, the exaggerated colours on Mikaël/Laure's face: the blusher, the eye shadow, the lipstick. Their mother comments on how pretty they look, and Mikaël/Laure responds with an embarrassed shake of the head, lying down on the bed with their mother, both facing the camera. Mikaël/ Laure's face, and by extension their whole body, here "inhabit [a] space that [does] not extend their shape, or use objects that do not extend their reach. At this moment of failure, such objects 'point' somewhere else or they make what is 'here' become strange" (Ahmed 2006, 160). In other words, Lisa's attempts to dress Mikaël/Laure up "as a girl" through the use of makeup signals a failed orientation. When the mother forces her child to wear the blue dress, we are aware of the dissonance between the surface of the body and the surface of the objects with which it is being made to engage. A similar disjunct emerges here. We recognize Mikaël/Laure, of course, but we also recognize this as a presentation other than that they choose for themselves and as a presentation that seems, by this stage in the film, to be an act of misgendering, not because we have decided Mikaël/Laure is a boy but because this is not how they present as a child.

Textures of Transformation

In some instances, it is not only a case of surfaces and textures being experienced, of the surfaces of children's bodies interacting physically with, and responding to, their lived environment. Rather, we understand that these surfaces and textures can also contribute to Mikaël/Laure's engagement with their own body – their desire to transform it or, indeed, to resist its transformation. The most obvious example of this arises in the Play-Doh penis sequence, which, it seems to me, is all about materiality and surfaces and a desire to shape and mould one's own surface, that which tends towards the world, in a way that stakes a claim for occupying a place within that world on one's own terms. The construction of the penis is very clearly about Mikaël/Laure wanting their body to look a certain way – and to *not* look another way – in the specific context of the children's swimming trip to the lake. We do not necessarily get the sense that the penis is now going to be something Mikaël/Laure wears every time they go out with their friends. It serves a specific and practical purpose that absolutely has to do with bodily transformation and, in particular, the desire to transform their silhouette, the shape they fill in the world. And as if to emphasize that it is not about to become an omnipresent feature of their appearance, we see Mikaël/Laure placing the Play-Doh penis in the little box they also use to keep their milk teeth. For the present moment, it has served its purpose.

The Play-Doh penis is not the only means by which the surfaces, textures, and materiality of childhood are queered in order to enable the characters to adapt their identity. We can also return here to the scene where Jeanne trims her sibling's hair. That is, of course, a scene that is about pretence, creativity, putting on voices, and the hilarity children find in addressing each other as they think adults speak ("Madame ..."), made all the more joyously fun because they are doing things their parents are unaware of here. The ticklish texture of the hair is an important part of the scene, too, though: we see Jeanne unable to keep her little hair-cutting moustache sitting on her top lip and Mikaël/Laure get tired of their moustache and twitch their nose and face to get rid of it, wiping away final traces with their hand. Hair is not just a part of Mikaël/Laure's body; it is a part of their body that they feel and engage with, a part of their body that reminds *us* of their embodiedness. Hair can contribute to a reshaping of self, in the very light-hearted way with the fake moustaches but also in the first bathroom scene, much earlier, when Jeanne insists on putting Mikaël/Laure's hair into a punk spike (as pretty much every child must have tried to do at some point). There, too, although very little is made of the action, we nevertheless hear Mikaël/Laure talking about how it *feels*, making clear that the crest is about to topple over.

Writing about Andrei Tarkovsky's 1975 film *Mirror*, Jennifer Barker observes that its characters' "embodied, emotional experiences may begin in and on the surface of the body, but they come to involve the entire body, and to register as movement, comportment, tension, internal rhythms, and a full-bodied engagement with the materiality of the world" (2009, 2). I suggest that we are watching a very similar process in *Tomboy*. So much of what we have seen Mikaël/Laure do, of how we have seen them interact with the world around them and with the other children, has come through their embodied engagement with the textures, surfaces, and materiality of that context. This engagement demonstrates that "bodies as well as objects take shape through being orientated toward each other, as an orientation that may be experienced as the co-habitation or sharing of space" (Ahmed 2006, 54). We have watched them negotiate a space for themselves, queering the very stuff of their childhood as they make their way through and in the world.

Conclusion

Reflecting on *Tomboy* more than a decade after its release has been an odd experience in many ways, not least because of the monumental transformation of Céline Sciamma's profile that was triggered by the release and reception of *Portrait de la jeune fille en feu* in 2019. Sciamma's political engagements and the cementing of her position not only within a contemporary French *cinematic* landscape but also in broader popular culture terms are now, of course, also part of how I watch *Tomboy*. As Ginette Vincendeau has noted, "It would be … premature to see the fact that Sciamma is officially 'out' in mainstream cultural media such as *Le Monde* in addition to lesbian publications as indicating that queer sexuality has become totally uncontroversial in France" (2022, 240).

Nevertheless, the very fact that Sciamma can be described as "the most visible and important feminist, and lesbian, director in international filmmaking at this moment" (Wilson 2021, 1) while also expressing her delight that the "respect" shown to *Portrait de la jeune fille en feu* "can help give credit to queer storytellers" (Crosara 2021) suggests Sciamma's determined insistence that categories be open to self-definition and self-identification. So, too, does the fact that she can confidently state that "the label of 'lesbian' is only restrictive if you think our imaginations are small" (Christopher 2020) while speaking of her desire to create "a queer love story with equality" in *Portrait* (Bordages 2019). This resonates with Wilson's suggestion that Sciamma seeks "not to circumscribe ... gender performance as child's play or make believe, nor to limit the film to a lesbian rather than trans reading, but to champion the fluid identifications and gender performances of childhood" (2021, 47). For me, Sciamma's claiming of the label of "queer filmmaker" without relinquishing the specificities of *lesbian* filmmaker is hugely significant, as I discussed in the introduction, because of its determination to counteract the potential erasure of lesbian identities by seeking to maintain it on equal footing with queer experiences, and thus speaks to the legitimacy of her place, and that of *Tomboy*, within the Queer Film Classics series.

And yet, beyond considering what makes Sciamma a queer director, my overriding recollection of my feelings after I first watched the film remains one of joy, and I very much hope I have offered a glimpse of that joy in these pages. It was a joyful experience to spend the best part of eighty minutes with a group of kids who were trying to figure out their place in the world. I feel joy when I hear the pop synths of Para One's "Always" beginning to play and find myself, a non-dancer, wanting to bop a little in my seat. And there is joy at having watched the story of a queer kid who reaches the end of a film in one piece. That might seem like a pretty low bar, but the significance not of a *happy* ending but of an open ending that seems to be so filled with queer possibilities cannot be understated.

Tomboy is, in many ways, a "light" film. It is comparatively short, low-key, intimate, and luminous. It is not a film that wallows in its subject matter, nor does it seek to psychologize or pathologize the actions and experiences of its central character, Mikaël/Laure. However, its lightness belies its multilayered and multitextured approach to questions of gendered identity, whose presence onscreen remains comparatively unusual. And it is in the film's multilayered and multitextured aesthetic and narrative choices that the film's queerness lies and that earns it the label of "queer film classic."

Tomboy is queer in its orientation, in its willingness – indeed, its determination – to consider queer lives at child height through its depiction of Mikaël/Laure's first summer holidays in their new home. Its narrative focus allows us to get to know Mikaël/Laure "unmoored" from the classroom's social conventions while nevertheless navigating the codes and conventions of gender within the microcosm of their peer group and family. And there is no rounded, closed conclusion to the filmic narrative. This strategy unmoors the viewer, in a sense, leaving us with a replay of an opening scene, an introduction to "Laure" and the beginning of a smile on a child's face, perhaps triggered by having the opportunity to introduce themselves again. For all the film may be "so brief and fleeting … it leaves no doubt that whether living as Laure or Mikaël, this child will grow up queer or trans" (Wilson 2021, 45). Sciamma does not suggest a blank canvas, in the sense that what came before has been erased, but rather the sketches of Mikaël/Laure's identity composed over the course of the summer underpin a conscious decision to self-name, to reinscribe oneself within a relationship, to resume a friendship in a "powerfully affirmative stance" (Lindner 2018, 203), a "mutual acknowledgement that queers both characters" (Lindner 2018, 222).

Where the queering lies, I argue, is in the replaying of the scene, in Sciamma's explicit desire to let Mikaël/Laure take the lead at the beginning and end of the narrative, to give them space to answer the simplest of children's questions: "What's your name?" The first time around, this question is preceded by Lisa's gendering of the new arrival as male. By the end of the film, in the closing seconds, as the scene plays out again the day before school resumes, there is no gendering via language that either precedes the question or is contained within it. The exchange opens up a world of new queer possibilities. A question; the space for a response; a response; a silence; the flicker of a smile from Mikaël/Laure. And we cut to the credits.

Notes

Chapter One

1 Details relating to awards and nominations are primarily taken from IMDb, last consulted on 2 August 2024.

2 All translations from French-language press reviews and articles are by the author.

3 Chevalier's reference to this process as a "superimposition" of identities is also significant in relation to much of what I will discuss in the final chapter, in particular, when I consider Sciamma's use of textures, materials, and surfaces in the film.

4 "I picked the title *Girlhood* not knowing *Boyhood* existed, but I was so glad" (Sciamma cited in *The Independent* 2015).

5 See, for example, "Céline Sciamma Interview: Step Aside 'Boyhood,' It's Time for 'Girlhood'" (*The Independent* 2015) or "TIFF Trailer: Céline Sciamma's 'Girlhood' is the Anti-'Boyhood'" (Lattanzio 2014).

6 Espineira defines "transidentité" as "an umbrella term under which transsexual and transgender individuals, as well as those with alternative trans identities, can recognise themselves" (2014, 1).

7 Espineira argues that, until 2018, the "rare trans characters in series and fictions were apolitical, mature, white, heterosexual women, 'husbands and fathers' before transitioning" (2021).

8 The central figures in these two films are, nevertheless, a couple of years younger than Mikaël/Laure. In *Ma Vie en rose* Ludo is seven (though the actor playing him was twelve when the film was shot) and Sasha in *Petite fille* is eight. A handful of other recent French-language films have also examined similar questions but with teenage or late-teen central figures, including the Belgian-French drama *Lola vers la mer* (Micheli, 2019) and Lukas Dhont's films *Girl* (2018) and *Close* (2022).

9 I would also note in passing here that, while the gender nonconformist child can be described as a "relatively recent addition," the children who *do* begin to appear in such narratives tend to be boys who want to be girls or who present as girls (see Waldron 2013, for example, for further discussion of this point). *Tomboy* is different because we are watching a (biological) girl who presents as a boy. In a more recent context, it would be interesting to compare the representation of self-transformation in *Tomboy* with that of the central child, Joe (Sasha Knight), in Anna Kerrigan's 2020 film *Cowboys*.

10 Numerous reviews published in France on the film's release in 2011 either used the French equivalent phrase "garçon manqué" in their headline, thus translating the film's title without having to do so explicitly, or found ways to use "garçon manqué" as part of a play on words. See, for example, Frois (2011), with "*Tomboy*, un film réussi pour un garçon manqué" (*Tomboy*, hit film for a failed boy); *Le Parisien* (2011) with "*Tomboy*, garçon manqué, film réussi" (*Tomboy*, a failed boy, a hit film); or Machart (2015) with the same title as *Le Parisien* but this time in *Le Monde*.

11 There is no explicit indication in the dialogue as to whether Jeanne's account is imagined or really took place. However, given the fallout from Lisa's calling to look for "Mikaël" and the multiple opportunities in the exchange between Mikaël/Laure and Jeanne for the latter to have made reference to this happening *again*, for example, I think we can assume that the story Jeanne tells Cheyenne is an imagined account.

12 Those who have seen *Naissance des pieuvres* may be reminded of the scene in Floriane's bedroom when she and Marie lie on the bed together. Floriane has asked Marie to "prepare" her for sleeping with François by "rather clinically" helping her lose her virginity (Chevalier 2019, 66) so the context for the sequence is highly significant. However, as is often the case in Sciamma, that significance is simultaneously emphasized and undercut by the incongruity of what is also happening. In this instance, for example, the scene veers toward the absurd as Marie is wearing the sequined swimming costume Floriane has given her as a gift *over* her own clothes and she starts to speculate about what must go through a fly's mind when it hits a car windscreen. For much of this exchange, Floriane and Marie are framed in the same way as Jeanne and Mikaël/Laure in *Tomboy*, where the gravity is also similarly undercut by the children's conversation centring not on their experience of their circumstances, nor their shock at their mother's act of violence, but instead taking the shape of a rather incongruous game of Who Am I?

13 Although it focuses on plot and actors, rather than explicitly listing lesbian directors, the annotated filmography in the groundbreaking *Sapphism on Screen* by Lucille Cairns (2006) is well worth reading for a sense of the landscape of lesbian filmmaking in France and the wider Francophone world.

14 In global box office terms, *Portrait* was the French film with the largest audience in cinemas worldwide in 2020, with 1.5 million viewers (Cojean 2021).

15 Without wishing to be too flippant, as though admission to the *Petit Robert* were insufficient in and of itself, in 2020 the term "queer" was also recognized as being acceptable for use in French Scrabble, a marker of linguistic shifts if nothing else (see http://1mot.net). On the other hand, a quick search through the online dictionary of the Académie Française, the body that has been policing French linguistic usage since the end of the seventeenth century, comes up with a rather definitive "No results found."

16 *Tomboy* found itself directly caught up in the controversy when it was chosen to be screened in schools as part of the "École et cinéma" initiative, which had the backing of the Ministries for Education and Culture. *Tomboy*'s inclusion triggered complaints from parents and a petition launched by the ultra-conservative organization Citizengo, which gathered more than 15,000 signatures (Doiezie 2013).

17 Naming strategies and the significance of taking ownership of one's name are also key in *Bande de filles* and *Portrait de la jeune fille en feu*. In the former, Lady renames Marième, the central character, Vic, another member of the "bande." Lady also offers Marième a necklace with the word "Vic," which marks the importance of this renaming. In *Portrait de la jeune fille en feu*, one of the markers of the horizontal solidarity that emerges between the three central characters (who in principle at least represent very different social classes) comes through their use of first names with each other. The significance of forms of address is also clear in *Portrait* when Héloïse and Marianne's sexual relationship begins and their customary use of the formal "vous" form with each other slips on a small number of occasions into use of the informal or familiar "tu," indicating the trust and love that has developed between them.

18 It is interesting to note that, even in her own linguistic usage at the time of *Tomboy*'s release, Sciamma often talks about the central character as female, using feminine pronouns, and describing her as "une petite fille" (a little girl, for example, in Dokhan 2011).

19 "Iel" started to be used in the early 2010s but only in October 2021 did the editors of the *Petit Robert* dictionary announce that they would be including it in their digital edition (Sorbier 2021).

20 We might think of a parallel here with the English-language question often posed of the parents of a new baby: "Is it a boy or a girl?" We can still balk at the binary, but at least options are provided such that neither gender is foregrounded.

21 Karine Chevalier signals a further way in which we can find approaches developed more fully in *Tomboy* already present in Sciamma's first film when she notes that, in *Naissance des pieuvres*, "the characters' feelings are first and foremost conveyed by their bodies and actions, rather than through dialogue" (2019, 64).

22 Spellings of the central character's name vary across different sources and I have opted simply to replicate the spellings used in particular articles or reviews while sticking with "Mikaël/Laure" myself.

23 Ironically, this lack of a non-gender-specific equivalent to "them" or "they" in French can also be seen in the French-language title of the American film *They* by Anahita Ghazvinizadeh (2017), the story of a fourteen-year-old trans teenager living in Chicago, which became *Il ou elle* (*He or She*) in French.

24 A term Sciamma uses herself in one interview (see Pellen 2011).

25 Sciamma herself also plays a small onscreen role in *Naissance des pieuvres*, appearing as a server in a McDonald's where Marie and Anne try to buy a Happy Meal.

26 There is an irony in Sciamma's choice of Demy insofar as she spoke in one interview (Vallet 2021) about the fact that, had she chosen an actress like Karin Viard to play the mother, audiences would only have seen the actress. Demy's cinematic lineage does not seem to have caused Sciamma the same concerns.

27 The reference to "the young team" makes even more sense when we consider that Acquart was sixteen, Haenel and Blachère were both nineteen, and Sciamma herself was only twenty-eight.

28 The term "banlieue" refers in spatial and geographical terms to the suburbs of Paris and other major French cities. However, more often than not it is used to evoke not only a specific architectural backdrop (high-rise apartment blocks, for example) but also a set of social and economic conditions. The so-called "*banlieue* cinema" emerged in the mid-1990s with the release of Mathieu Kassovitz's *La Haine* (*Hate*)

(1995). *Naissance des pieuvres* and *Tomboy*, with their quiet visions of suburbia, would not typically be identified as *banlieue* films, whereas *Bande de filles* engages with more of the tropes associated with the genre.

29 All translations from Barlet's interview with Niang and Nielsen are my own.

30 The term made its way into mainstream cultural debate in France around the release of the film, as well as through the work of Iris Brey, an author and journalist who published *Le Regard féminin* in 2020. Brey observed that *Portrait*'s emblematic status as a film of the "female gaze" stems from the fact that, in Sciamma's film, the notion of desire emerges from the notion of equality: "It is very rare to see a film in which two people, indeed two women, learn to love each other while regarding each other as equals" (Brey cited in Veunac 2021).

31 Sciamma was the first woman to receive it. French lesbian film director Catherine Corsini was the 2021 recipient, for *La Fracture* (*The Divide*).

32 A hugely controversial piece of legislation adopted by the French Parliament in April 2021. The key source of the controversy stemmed from Article 24 of the law, which makes it an offence to "provocatively" identify police officers. But the overall tenure of the legislation was also deeply problematic and seen by many as formalizing a culture of surveillance, particularly around demonstrations. Haenel and Beausson-Diagne both demonstrated against the legislation in Paris a few days before the Mediapart interview.

33 The examples I mention here all centre on Sciamma and Haenel, whose personal relationship – and, in the case of Haenel, the increased visibility following her public statements about Ruggia – has highlighted their political engagement in the past couple of years. However, Noémie Merlant and Luana Bajrami have also continued to take a stance on questions of gender and sexual politics and much was made of the support the quartet demonstrated for each other's work at

Cannes 2021 where Bajrami and Merlant both had directorial roles. Bajrami's first film as director (*La Colline où rugissent les lionnes* [*The Hill Where Lionesses Roar*]) was shown as part of the Quinzaine des Réalisateurs while Merlant's full-length debut as director (*Mi Iubita, Mon Amour*) was also screened at the festival. Sciamma, meanwhile, attended as screenwriter on Jacques Audiard's *Les Olympiades*, which stars Merlant, while Haenel is the narrator of Jean-Gabriel Périot's screen adaptation of Didier Eribon's 2009 memoir *Retour à Reims* (*Returning to Reims (Fragments)*, 2021). The collaborative exchanges have continued and *Les Femmes au balcon* (*The Balconettes*), which Merlant and Sciamma co-wrote and Merlant directed, was screened at Cannes in 2024.

34 The intertextuality of the cultural moment can also be seen in placards that declared "On se lève et on se barre" (We're getting up and we're getting out). The reference is to the open letter Virgine Despentes wrote and published under the same title in *Libération* on 1 March 2020, saluting Haenel's departure from the César ceremony. Despentes ends her text in no uncertain terms: "We're getting up and we're leaving. It's finished. We're getting up. We're leaving. We're shouting. We say, 'screw you.'"

35 Estimates suggest that between 400 and 500 full-length features were in line for possible release when French screens reopened (Caron 2021).

36 While Sciamma talks about her desire to avoid including this nostalgic gaze in the film, some press coverage and published interviews reveal a certain nostalgia for childhood. In Pryor (2011), for instance, she is asked to what extent the film draws on her own life and responds: "I wasn't looking for the ambiguity as a child, it was just the era – lots of little girls really had short hair in the 80s. There was more androgyny back then, and I think childhood lasted longer at that time. I think I was a child at 12-years-old, which seems amazing today."

37 It has cropped up again in mainstream coverage of Sciamma's most recent film to date, *Petite Maman*. See, for example, Cojean (2021), while Clarisse Fabre observed that it took "Céline Sciamma's gaze to turn a film shot at child height into a fantastic, or even metaphysical, tale" (2023) and Marc Arlin described the film as "a lovely tale shot at child height" in *Télé-Loisirs* (2021). Indeed, in relation to *Petite Maman*, Sciamma's cinematographer Claire Mathon noted that working "at child height was important, but working at the height of [the central character] Nelly's imagination was too" (Webb 2021).

38 It is also a phrase that we see recurring in reviews of *Ma Vie de Courgette*, the stop motion animation film written by Sciamma and directed by Claude Barras. See, for example, "*Ma Vie de Courgette*, un grand film d'animation à hauteur d'enfant" (A great animated film at child's height [Odicino 2016] – the French plays on the ambiguity of the adjective "grand" here, which can mean either "great" or "tall"/"big").

39 "Céline Sciamma never looks on her subject from the perspective of an adult observing childhood from on high" (Marceau 2011, n.p.).

40 I would suggest that there is a useful parallel to observe here between *Tomboy* and the earlier *Ma Vie en rose*, insofar as both films allow their central child figure the scope to be unmoored, unanchored from the physical world (albeit in different ways). With Sciamma this comes through a positioning of Mikaël/Laure at an unusual – more often than not, elevated – angle in relation to the world around them, shifting the position from which we expect a child to gaze on their environment. With Berliner, on the other hand, a similar effect is achieved through the fantasy sequences when Ludo drifts off into reveries about his favorite soap opera characters, Pam and Ben, and imagines himself to be floating above the world. While Sciamma tends to follow such sequences in *Tomboy* with scenes of inclusion, for Ludo these are very clearly *imagined* scenes and tend to be followed by sharp disjuncts with the codes and conventions of their immediate environment.

41 Sciamma's depiction of the banlieue housing scheme in *Bande de filles* also uses horizontality in its framing in ways that stand out from other films in the loose "cinéma de banlieue" category, focusing more on shots of Marième (and other characters) wandering along walkways and corridors, looking out across a horizon, walking along the side of a building, than on shots of high-rise blocks that emphasize their verticality. We see that kind of verticality, for example, in Kassovitz's *La Haine* (1995) and in Zeitoun and Seri's 2001 parkour banlieue film *Yamakasi – Les Samouraïs des temps modernes*.

Chapter Two

1 On Sciamma's own account, a key exception to the spontaneity came in the Truth or Dare sequence in which she recounts that every question and every response was, in fact, fed to the children, rather than being the product of their own imaginations (Jeamart 2011).
2 Sciamma has subsequently explored the imaginative territory of the forest and of the forest clearing more fully in *Petite Maman*, shooting the film in the same woods she had played in as a child (Lannoy 2021).
3 We can also, of course, consider the disembodiment of the mother's voice in this key scene as another strategy employed by Sciamma to keep the children centre-stage and the adults on the periphery.
4 Full lyrics can be found online (see "Mamalisa's World" 2021).
5 Writing in *Le Monde*, for example, Jean-Luc Douin (2011) notes that "the mystery is lifted when Michaël gets out of the bath. Michaël is a girl," while Gérard Lefort (2011), referring to the same scene, simply states: "When Michaël gets home, as his mother says, it's Laure. Like a girl." Neither makes any further reference to the scene and most reviews simply make no reference to this specific scene.

Chapter Three

1 There is a lovely irony in reading the opening scene in *Tomboy* as a key example of haptic cinema, as defined by Laura Marks, while the latter simultaneously notes that "a certain degree of separation from the body is necessary in order for our bodies to function … If we were aware of the functioning of our spleens, the constant activity upon the mucous membranes of our nostrils, the traffic on our synaptic highways, *we would certainly not be able to drive a car*, let alone distinguish perceptions most necessary for survival" (2000, 132, my italics).

2 Swimming also features in the opening ten minutes of Sciamma's *Portrait de la jeune fille en feu*, of course, as we see Marianne, the painter, the only passenger in a rowing boat, accompanied most notably by a large wooden crate. The boat is rocked by a large wave that sends the crate over the edge and into the water and Marianne, fully dressed and yet to utter a word, dives in to retrieve it. She drags it back onboard and sits shivering for the rest of the journey in her soaking clothes, hunched over herself in much the same way as we see Mikaël/Laure hunched up and shivering on the diving platform in *Tomboy* and, indeed, as we have seen Marie shivering with cold in the changing rooms in *Naissance des pieuvres*.

3 The inevitability of the new school year and what that means for Mikaël/Laure's presentation of self is also clear when their mother learns what is happening and drags her child to other children's homes. Mikaël/Laure is desperate not to go and they stop in the walkways of the apartment block where the mother asks if they have another solution, explaining that she does not and that, because school will soon begin, they "must" do this.

4 While the French verb "se déguiser" can be used to mean "to disguise oneself," I would argue that term normally suggests deliberate subterfuge and, perhaps more importantly, someone who is being tricked

by the disguise. There is no implication in this scene that Lisa or Mikaël/Laure intend to trick anyone. Moreover, in terms of common French usage, "se déguiser" would be the obvious verbal choice for kids talking about dressing up (rather than *disguising* themselves). We can also consider the language here in parallel with an exchange between Mikaël/Laure and their mother, after the latter has learned that "Laure" is also passing as "Mikaël." She asks her child whether they plan to pass themselves off as a boy all year long ("tu vas te faire passer pour un garçon"), before telling Mikaël/Laure that she doesn't mind if they want to "play at being a boy" (jouer au garçon).

5 We can see here an illustration of Waldron's suggestion that "of all the children, including Laure, [Lisa] is the most queerly constructed," insofar as she is simultaneously "tomboyish" and "a narrative agent" as well as "recognizing Laure's different early on" (2013, 70).

References

1mot.net. 2020. "Le mot 'queer' est valide au Scrabble." https://1mot.net/queer.

Académie française. 2022. *Dictionnaire de l'Académie française*. Digital edition. https://www.dictionnaire-academie.fr/presentation.

Ahmed, Sara. 2006. *Queer Phenomenology: Orientations, Objects, Others*. Durham and London: Duke University Press.

Anderson, Melissa. 2011. "Tween Choice: Complicating Late Childhood in Tomboy." *Village Voice*, 16 November. https://www.villagevoice.com/2011/11/16/tween-choice-complicating-late-childhood-in-tomboy/.

Arlin, Marc. 2021. "Petite Maman: Céline Sciamma signe un joli conte à hauteur d'enfant." Télé-Loisirs, 2 December. https://www.programme-tv.net/news/cinema/288613-petite-maman-canal-cinema-celine-sciamma-signe-un-joli-conte-a-hauteur-denfant/.

Barker, Jennifer. 2009. *The Tactile Eye*. Berkeley: University of California Press.

Barlet, Olivier. 2018. "Si on est là, c'est qu'on est résilientes, on va continuer!" *Africultures: Les Mondes en relation*, 28 March. http://africultures.com/on-cest-quon-resilientes-on-va-continuer-14426/.

Baurez, Thomas. 2011. "Tomboy, du cinéma beau et puissant." *L'Express*, 19 April. https://www.lexpress.fr/culture/cinema/tomboy_982484.html.

Berger, Katia. 1997. "Petit garçon deviendra fille ... Conte de la différence, ode à la tolérance." *Journal de Genève*, 31 May. https://alainberliner.com/site/wp-content/uploads/2011/05/presse-FR.pdf.

Berlinale. 2020. "Petite Fille." https://www.berlinale.de/en/2020/programme/202010327.html.

Bond-Stockton, Kathryn. 2009. *The Queer Child or Growing Sideways in the Twentieth Century*. Durham: Duke University Press.

Bordages, Anaïs. 2019. "Céline Sciamma: 'Il y a eu un sacrifice de lesbiennes dans toute l'histoire du cinéma.'" *Slate.fr*, 4 June. https://www.slate.fr/story/177996/portrait-de-la-jeune-fille-en-feu-celine-sciamma-film-romantique-politique.

Bradbury-Rance, Clara. 2019. *Lesbian Cinema after Queer Theory*. Edinburgh: Edinburgh University Press.

Bradfer, Fabienne. 1997. "Ma Vie en rose. Féroce, tendre et généreux. À voir." *Le Soir*, 28 May. https://alainberliner.com/site/wp-content/uploads/2011/05/presse-FR.pdf.

Brady, Tara. 2011. "Tomboy." *Irish Times*, 16 September. https://www.irishtimes.com/culture/film/tomboy-1.601682.

Brey, Iris. 2018. "Cannes 2018: récit de l'intérieur de la montée des marches en faveur de la parité au cinéma." *Les Inrockuptibles*, 15 May. https://www.lesinrocks.com/cinema/cannes-2018-recit-de-linterieur-de-la-monte-des-marches-en-faveur-de-la-parite-au-cinema-143421-15-05-2018/.

– 2020. *Le Regard féminin*. Paris: Éditions de l'Olivier.

Caillard, Frédéric. 2011. "Qu'est-ce que sexe? Tomboy de Céline Sciamma." *Critikat*, 19 April 2011. https://www.critikat.com/actualite-cine/critique/tomboy/.

Cairns, Lucille. 2006. *Sapphism on Screen: Lesbian Desire in French and Francophone Cinema*. Edinburgh: Edinburgh University Press.

Caron, Christophe. 2021. "Réouverture des salles le 19 mai: le cinéma français en tête de gondole." *La Voix du Nord*, 29 April. https://www.lavoix

dunord.fr/993682/article/2021-04-29/reouverture-des-salles-le-19-mai-le-cinema-francais-tete-de-gondole.

Chareyron, Romain, and Gilles Viennot. 2019. "Disparate Lives: Representations of Youth in French and Francophone Cinema." In *Screening Youth: Contemporary French and Francophone Cinema*, edited by Romain Chareyron and Gilles Viennot, 1–17. Edinburgh: Edinburgh University Press.

Chevalier, Karine. 2019. "Repetition and Difference: The Representation of Youth in the Films of Céline Sciamma." In *Screening Youth: Contemporary French and Francophone Cinema*, edited by Romain Chareyron and Gilles Viennot, 62–80. Edinburgh: Edinburgh University Press.

Christopher, Megan. 2020. "Portrait of a Lady on Fire: Céline Sciamma on Lesbian Identity." *Screen Queens*, 28 February. https://screenqueens.wordpress.com/2020/02/28/portrait-of-a-lady-on-fire-talking-to-celine-sciamma-about-lesbian-identity/.

Cojean, Annick. 2021. "Céline Sciamma: 'S'engager rend toujours vulnérable.'" *Le Monde*, 6 June. https://www.lemonde.fr/culture/article/2021/06/06/celine-sciamma-s-engager-rend-toujours-vulnerable_6083033_3246.html.

Crosara, Nic. 2021. "The Director of *Portrait of a Lady on Fire* Is Back with Another Masterpiece." *Diva Magazine*, November. https://diva-magazine.com/2021/11/19/celine-sciamma-on-petite-maman-the-kid-gaze-and-queer-cinema/.

Dargis, Manohla. 2011. "A Summer of Freedoms in Boyhood." *New York Times*, 15 November. https://www.nytimes.com/2011/11/16/movies/tomboy-by-celine-sciamma-review.html.

Daumas, Cécile, Rachid Laïreche, and Sandra Onana. 2020. "Aïssa Maïga et Adèle Haenel: 'Enfin il se passe un truc politique.'" *Libération*, 12 June. https://www.liberation.fr/cinema/2020/06/12/pourquoi-ne-se-pense-t-on-pas-comme-des-allies-spontanes-et-necessaires_1791150/.

De Bruyn, Olivier. 2011. "'Tomboy' – une merveille de sensibilité." *Le Point*, 18 April. https://www.lepoint.fr/cinema/tomboy-une-merveille-de-sensibilite-18-04-2011-1320578_35.php.

De Kervasdoué, Cécile. 2021. "L'écriture inclusive, un débat très politique." *France Culture*, 9 May. https://www.franceculture.fr/politique/lecriture-inclusive-un-debat-tres-politique.

Despentes, Virginie. 2020. "Désormais on se lève et on se barre." *Libération*, 1 March. https://www.liberation.fr/debats/2020/03/01/cesars-desormais-on-se-leve-et-on-se-barre_1780212/.

Diatkine, Anne. 2011. "Tomboy: L'avis du Elle." *Elle*, 27 April. https://www.elle.fr/Loisirs/Cinema/Films/Tomboy.

Dodman, Benjamin. 2021. "'Françaises, Français': Could the French Language Be Less Sexist?" *France24*, 25 February. https://www.france24.com/en/culture/20210225-fran%C3%A7aises-fran%C3%A7ais-why-the-french-language-need-not-be-so-sexist.

Doiezie, Mathilde. 2013. "Tomboy: sa projection controversée dans les écoles." *Le Figaro*, 24 December. https://www.lefigaro.fr/cinema/2013/12/24/03002-20131224ARTFIG00339—tomboy-sa-projection-controversee-dans-les-ecoles.php.

Dokhan, Julien. 2011. "Tomboy: Interview avec Céline Sciamma." *AlloCiné*, 20 April. http://www.allocine.fr/article/fichearticle_gen_carticle=18603428.html.

Douin, Jean-Luc. 2011. "'Tomboy': Malentendus identitaires." *Le Monde*, 19 April. https://www.lemonde.fr/cinema/article/2011/04/19/malentendus-identitaires_1509887_3476.html.

Duong, Kevin. 2014. "Gender Trouble in France: An Interview with Camille Robcis." *Jacobin*, 8 December. https://jacobin.com/2014/12/gender-trouble-in-france/.

Ebert, Roger. 2012. "This May Frame Her Adulthood, or Just Be Forgotten." 25 January. https://www.rogerebert.com/reviews/tomboy-2012.

Edney, Gemma. 2019. "Un Vrai 'Teen Film' Français? The Contemporary

Adolescent Genre in French Cinema." In *Screening Youth: Contemporary French and Francophone Cinema*, edited by Romain Chareyron and Gilles Viennot, 18–32. Edinburgh: Edinburgh University Press.

EFA (European Film Awards). 2011. *Tomboy*. https://europeanfilmawards.eu/en_EN/film/tomboy.5305.

English, Jeri. 2019. "Childhood and Gender Panic in *Ma Vie en rose* and *Tomboy*." In *Screening Youth: Contemporary French and Francophone Cinema*, edited by Romain Chareyron and Gilles Viennot, 33–46. Edinburgh: Edinburgh University Press.

Éribon, Didier. 2009. *Retour à Reims*. Paris: Fayard.

Espineira, Karine. 2021. "Les Personnages trans dans les séries françaises." *Le Genre et l'écran*, 31 October. https://www.genre-ecran.net/?Les-personnages-trans-dans-les-series-francaises.

– 2014. "La sexualité des sujets transgenres et transsexuels saisie par les médias." Hermès, La Revue – Cognition, Communication, Politique, CNRS-Éditions: 105–9.

Euzen, Philippe. 2014. "'L'ABCD de l'égalité,' au cœur de la polémique sur la 'théorie du genre.'" *Le Monde*, 31 January. https://www.lemonde.fr/politique/article/2014/01/31/qu-est-ce-que-l-abcd-de-l-egalite_4358081_823448.html.

Fabre, Charlie. 2022. "Trans Kids in France: Unpacking the Media Frenzy." In *Trans Identities in the French Media: Representation, Visibility, Recognition*, edited by Romain Chareyron, 23–42. Lanham and London: Rowman & Littlefield.

Fabre, Clarisse. 2021. "Petite Maman, ou l'art de retrouver sa mère." *Le Monde*, 31 May. https://www.lemonde.fr/culture/article/2021/05/31/petite-maman-ou-l-art-de-retrouver-sa-mere_6082275_3246.html.

– 2023. "Petite Maman sur France 4: rencontre du 'troisième type' entre une petite fille et sa mère enfant." *Le Monde*, 26 May. https://www.lemonde.fr/culture/article/2023/05/26/petite-maman-sur-france-4-rencontre-du-troisieme-type-entre-une-petite-fille-et-sa-mere-enfant_6175024_3246.html.

France Inter. 2019. "Intérieur Queer." https://www.franceinter.fr/emissions/interieur-queer.

Frois, Emmanuèle. 2011. "'Tomboy,' un film réussi pour un garçon manqué." *Le Figaro*, 19 April. https://www.lefigaro.fr/cinema/2011/04/19/03002-20110419ARTFIG00377—tomboy-un-film-reussi-pour-un-garcon-manque.php.

Green, Steph. 2019. "Gender, Nature and Fluidity: Articulating Childhood in Céline Sciamma's Tomboy." *Screen Queens*, 21 June. https://screen-queens.com/2019/06/21/gender-nature-and-fluidity-articulating-childhood-in-celine-sciammas-tomboy/.

Gunther, Scott. 2008. *The Elastic Closet: A History of Homosexuality in France, 1942–Present*. Basingstoke and New York: Palgrave Macmillan.

Haenel, Adèle. 2023. "'J'ai décidé de politiser mon arrêt du cinéma': la lettre d'Adèle Haenel à Télérama." *Télérama*, 9 May. https://www.telerama.fr/debats-reportages/j-ai-decide-de-politiser-mon-arret-du-cinema-la-lettre-d-adele-haenel-a-telerama-7015465.php.

Halberstam, Jack. 2022. "Unbuilding Gender." In *Theories of Performance: Critical and Primary Sources*, edited by Kelina Gotman, vol. 4, 187–97. New York and London: Bloomsbury.

Halberstam, J. 2002. "An Introduction to Female Masculinity: Masculinity without Men." In *The Masculinity Studies Reader*, edited by Rachel Adams and David Savran, 355–74. Oxford: Blackwell.

– 1998. *Female Masculinity*. Durham and London: Duke University Press.

Handyside, Fiona. 2023. "From Sisterhood to Matrophobia: Reading the Family Romance in the Films of Céline Sciamma." *French Screen Studies* 23, no. 2–3: 159–71.

Hemelryk Donald, Stephanie, Emma Wilson, and Sarah Wright. 2018. "Introduction: Nation, Film, Child." In *Childhood and Nation in Contemporary World Cinema*, edited by Stephanie Hemelryk Donald, Emma Wilson, and Sarah Wright, 1–11. New York and London: Bloomsbury.

IMDb. No date. "Tomboy." Accessed 27 March 2025. https://www.imdb.com/title/tt1847731/.

The Independent. 2015. "Céline Sciamma Interview: Step Aside 'Boyhood,' It's 'Girlhood' Time." *Independent*, 24 April. https://www.independent.co.uk/arts-entertainment/films/celine-sciamma-interview-step-aside-boyhood-it-s-girlhood-time-10199093.html.

Jeamart, Audrey. 2011. "Filmer à hauteur d'enfant." *Critikat*, 3 May. https://www.critikat.com/panorama/entretien/celine-sciamma/.

Johnston, Cristina. 2021. "The Queer Circulation of Objects in the Films of Céline Sciamma." *French Screen Studies*. https://doi.org/10.1080/26438941.2021.1956717.

Jonet, M. Catherine. 2017. "Desire and Queer Adolescence: Céline Sciamma's Naissance des pieuvres." *Journal of Popular Culture* 50, issue 5: 1127–42.

Joseph-Gabriel, Annette. 2019. "Who Gets to Speak for Black French People?" 23 April. https://africasacountry.com/2019/04/who-gets-to-speak-for-black-french-people.

Kearney, Mary Celeste. 2007. "Productive Spaces: Girls' Bedrooms as Sites of Cultural Production." *Journal of Children and Media* 1, no. 2: 126–41.

Keslassy, Elsa. 2021. "MK2 Film Sparks Bidding War with Céline Sciamma's *Petite Maman*." *Variety*, 16 March. https://variety.com/2021/film/global/celine-sciamma-petite-maman-berlinale-mk2-sales-1234931830/.

Kermode, Mark. 2021. "Petite Maman Review – Céline Sciamma's Heartbreakingly Hopeful Fairytale for All Ages." *Observer*, 21 November. https://www.theguardian.com/film/2021/nov/21/petite-maman-review-celine-sciamma-heartbreakingly-hopeful-fairytale-for-all-ages.

Kilduff, Hannah. 2018. "'The Child as Hyphen: Yamina Benguigui's Inch'allah Dimanche." In *Childhood and Nation in Contemporary World Cinema*, edited by Stephanie Hemelryk Donald, Emma Wilson, and Sarah Wright, 200–14. New York and London: Bloomsbury.

Knight, Aimee. 2021. "Petite Maman." *Little White Lies*, 18 November. https://lwlies.com/reviews/petite-maman/.

Kosnick, Kiki. 2019. "The Everyday Poetics of Gender-Inclusive French: Strategies for Navigating the Linguistic Landscape." *Modern & Contemporary France* 27, issue 2: 147–61.

La Langue française. 2023. "Queer." Last updated 9 October 2023. https://www.lalanguefrancaise.com/dictionnaire/definition/queer.

Lachman, Kathryn M. 2023. "Wonder and Loss in Céline Sciamma's *Petite Maman*." *French Cultural Studies* 35, no. 3: 215–28.

Lalanne, Jean-Marc. 2011. "Tomboy, grand film de genres." *Les Inrockuptibles*, 19 April. https://www.lesinrocks.com/cinema/tomboy-grand-film-de-genres-22110-19-04-2011/.

Lannoy, Stéphanie. 2021. "'Le regard d'enfant est un regard perçant.' Céline Sciamma, *Petite Maman*." *Madame fait son cinéma*. https://madamefaitsoncinema.be/2021/06/26/le-regard-denfant-est-un-regard-percant-celine-sciamma-petite-maman/.

Lattanzio, Ryan. 2014. "TIFF Trailer: Céline Sciamma's 'Girlhood' Is the Anti-'Boyhood.'" *IndieWire*, 9 September. https://www.indiewire.com/2014/09/tiff-trailer-celine-sciammas-girlhood-is-the-anti-boyhood-191071/.

Lefort, Gérard. 2011. "Quelle Laure est-il?" *Libération*, 20 April. https://www.liberation.fr/cinema/2011/04/20/quelle-laure-est-il_730226/.

Libiot, Eric. 2011. "Tomboy, un beau film mais le DVD manque de suppléments." *L'Express*, 28 September. https://www.lexpress.fr/culture/cinema/tomboy_1034518.html.

Lindner, Katharina. 2018. *Film Bodies: Queer Feminist Encounter with Gender and Sexuality in Cinema*. London/New York: I.B. Tauris.

LoopSider. 2021. "Qu'a fait Céline Sciamma du César d'honneur de Jeanne Moreau?" https://www.youtube.com/watch?v=akZYjGwfzv4.

Lussier, Marc-André. 2022. "Petit conte, grand film." *La Presse*, 13 May. https://www.lapresse.ca/cinema/critiques/2022-05-13/petite-maman/petit-conte-grand-film.php.

Machart, Renaud. 2015. "Tomboy, garçon manqué, film réussi." *Le Monde*, 17 November. https://www.lemonde.fr/televisions-radio/article/2015/11/20/tomboy-garcon-manque-film-reussi_4814104_1655027.html.

Mama Lisa's World. 2021. "Anatole, Monsieur Paul. Chanson enfantine." https://www.mamalisa.com/?t=fs&p=1418.

Marceau, Nicolas. 2011. "Androgyne taille basse. Entretien – Céline Sciamma." *L'Ouvreuse*, 28 April. http://louvreuse.net/Podcast/entretien-celine-sciamma.html.

Marks, Laura U. 2000. *The Skin of the Film: Intercultural Cinema, Embodiment, and the Senses*. Durham and London: Duke University Press.

Martin, Marie-Claude. 1997. "Dans tout ce noir, vive le pastel!" *Le Nouveau Quotidien*, 7 May. https://alainberliner.com/site/wp-content/uploads/2011/05/presse-FR.pdf.

Massonnat, François. 2022. "Petite Maman par Céline Sciamma (review)." *French Review* 96, no. 1: 284.

McRobbie, Angela, and Jenny Garber. 1976. "Girls and Subcultures." In *Resistance through Rituals: Youth Subcultures in Post-War Britain*, edited by Stuart Hall and Tony Jefferson, 209–22. London: Harper Collins Academic.

Nappey, Grégoire. 1997. "Tu seras un homme, mon fils." *La Presse Riviera-Chablais*, 6 June. https://alainberliner.com/site/wp-content/uploads/2011/05/presse-FR.pdf.

Odicino, Guillemette. 2011. "Trois questions à la réalisatrice de Tomboy, Céline Sciamma." *Télérama*, 29 June. https://www.telerama.fr/television/trois-questions-a-la-realisatrice-de-tomboy-celine-sciamma,83580.php.

– 2016. "Ma Vie de Courgette, un grand film d'animation à hauteur d'enfant." *Télérama*, 19 October. https://www.telerama.fr/cinema/ma-vie-de-courgette-un-grand-film-d-animation-a-hauteur-d-enfant,149033.php.

Le Parisien. 2011. "Tomboy, garçon manqué, film réussi." 20 April. https://www.leparisien.fr/culture-loisirs/tomboy-garcon-manque-film-reussi-20-04-2011-1415171.php.

Pellen, Guénola. 2011. "Tomboy, le sexe sans contrefaçon selon Céline Sciamma." 17 November. https://france-amerique.com/en/tomboy-le-sexe-sans-contrefacon-selon-celine-sciamma/.

Perreau, Bruno. 2018. *Qui a peur de la théorie queer?* Paris: Presses de Sciences Po.

Provencher, Denis M. 2007. *Queer French: Globalization, Language, and Sexual Citizenship in France*. Aldershot: Ashgate.

Pryor, John-Paul. 2011. "Céline Sciamma on Tomboy." *AnOther*, 28 September. https://www.anothermag.com/art-photography/1423/celine-sciamma-on-tomboy.

Reeser, Todd W. 2013. "Trans France." *L'Esprit Créateur* 53, no. 1: 4–14.

Saunders, Keeley. 2014. "Gender-Defined Spaces, Places and Tropes: Contemporary Transgender Representation in Tomboy and Romeos." *Journal of European Popular Culture* 5, issue 2: 181–93.

Schmitt, Amandine. 2018. "Queer, antisystème et rançongiciel entrent dans le dictionnaire." *Le Nouvel Obs*, 14 May. https://bibliobs.nouvelobs.com/actualites/20180514.OBS6605/queer-antisysteme-et-rancongiciel-entrent-dans-le-dictionnaire.html.

Sciamma, Céline, and Annie Ernaux. 2021. "Céline Sciamma et Annie Ernaux. Sœurs de combat." *La Déferlante*, no. 1 (March): 6–19.

Smith, Ellie. 2023. "'Des plafonds dans les yeux': Representing the New Town in *Naissance des pieuvres*." *French Screen Studies* 23, no. 2–3: 133–44.

Smith, Frances. 2023a. "The Films of Céline Sciamma: A Cinema of Youth and Desire." *French Screen Studies* 23, no. 2–3: 115–19.

– 2023b. "The Rules of the Game: Sports and the Gendered Body in Céline Sciamma's Youth Films." *French Screen Studies* 23, no. 2–3: 145–58.

Solal, Julien. 2011. "Tomboy. Une étude au scalpel de la psyché d'une enfant en mal d'identité." *L'Express*, 21 September. https://www.lexpress.fr/culture/cinema/tomboy_1032302.html.

Sorbier, Marie. 2021. "Le pronom 'iel' est une affaire linguistique en cours."

France Culture, 18 November. https://www.franceculture.fr/emissions/affaire-en-cours/l-entree-dans-le-dictionnaire-du-pronom-iel.

Trouillard, Gwenola. 2020. "Adèle Haenel: Une femme indignée." *Télé-Loisirs*, 19 May. https://www.programme-tv.net/news/cinema/254891-portrait-de-la-jeune-fille-en-feu-canal-qui-es-tu-adele-haenel/.

Turchi, Marine. 2024. "Affaire Adèle Haenel: le parquet demande un procès pour 'agressions sexuelles sur mineure.'" *Mediapart*, 8 February. https://www.mediapart.fr/journal/france/080224/affaire-adele-haenel-le-parquet-demande-un-proces-pour-agressions-sexuelles-sur-mineure.

Unifrance. 2022. "Petite Maman." https://www.unifrance.org/film/52040/petite-maman.

Vallet, Romain. 2012. "Céline Sciamma: 'Gamine, j'étais un peu un garçon manqué.'" *Hétéroclite*, 2 April. http://www.heteroclite.org/2012/04/interview-celine-sciamma-tomboy-lyon-1477.

Veunac, Caroline. 2021. "Iris Brey, pour un regard féminin au cinéma." *Centre Pompidou Magazine*, 18 February. https://www.centrepompidou.fr/en/magazine/article/iris-brey-pour-un-regard-feminin-au-cinema.

Vincendeau, Ginette. 2022. "Why Has Céline Sciamma Become So Iconic? The Auteure as Celebrity." *French Screen Studies* 23, no. 2–3: 231–47.

Waldron, Darren. 2013. "Embodying Gender Nonconformity in 'Girls': Céline Sciamma's Tomboy." *L'Esprit créateur* 53, no. 1: 60–73.

Webb, Oliver. 2021. "Claire Mathon, AFC, parle de Petite Maman de Céline Sciamma." 11 October. https://www.afcinema.com/Claire-Mathon-AFC-parle-de-Petite-maman-de-Celine-Sciamma.html.

Wilson, Emma. 2021. *Céline Sciamma: Portraits*. Edinburgh: Edinburgh University Press.

Women and Hollywood. 2011. "Interview with Céline Sciamma: Writer/Director of *Tomboy*." 15 November. https://womenandhollywood.com/interview-with-celine-sciamma-writer-director-of-tomboy-f3987112b60b/.

Woodward, Daisy. 2016. "Alison Watt's Beautiful Meditations on Fabric."

AnOther, 24 March. https://www.anothermag.com/art-photography/8516/alison-watts-beautiful-meditations-on-fabric.

Zafiris, Alex. 2015. "Céline Sciamma: Bande de filles." *Guernica*, 3 February. https://www.guernicamag.com/celine-sciamma-bande-de-filles/.

Zulueta, Ricardo E. 2012. "'Tomboy' (review)." *Film & History: An Interdisciplinary Journal* 42, no. 2 (Fall): 107–10.

Filmography

Alien. Ridley Scott, 1979, USA, 117 min.

L'Argent de poche (*Small Change*). François Truffaut, 1976, France, 104 min.

Bande de filles (*Girlhood*). Céline Sciamma, 2014, France, 113 min.

Boyhood. Richard Linklater, 2014, USA, 165 min.

Boys Don't Cry. Kimberley Peirce, 1999, USA, 118 min.

Close. Lukas Dhont, 2022, Belgium, 105 min.

La Colline où rugissent les lionnes (*The Hill Where Lionesses Roar*). Luana Bajrami, 2021, France/Kosovo, 83 min.

Cowboys. Anna Kerrigan, 2020, USA, 86 min.

Divines. Uda Benyamina, 2016, France, 105 min.

Documenteur. Agnès Varda, 1981, France, 65 min.

Edward Scissorhands. Tim Burton, 1990, USA, 105 min.

L'Effrontée (*An Impudent Girl*). Claude Miller, 1985, France, 96 min.

E.T. the Extra-Terrestrial. Steven Spielberg, 1982, USA, 115 min.

Les Femmes au balcon (*The Balconettes*). Noémie Merlant, 2024, France, 105 min.

La Fracture (*The Divide*). Catherine Corsini, 2021, France, 98 min.

Girl. Lukas Dhont, 2018, Belgium, 106 min.

La Haine (*Hate*). Mathieu Kassovitz, 1995, France, 98 min.

Jane B. par Agnès V. Agnès Varda, 1988, France, 99 min.

Kung-fu Master. Agnès Varda, 1988, France, 80 min.

Lola vers la mer (*Lola and the Sea*). Laurent Micheli, 2019, Belgium/France, 90 min.

Ma Vie de Courgette (*My Life as a Courgette*). Claude Barras, 2016, France/Switzerland, 66 min.

Ma Vie en rose (*My Life in Pink*). Alain Berliner, 1997, Belgium/France/UK, 88 min.

Mariannes noires. Mame-Fatou Niang and Kaytie Nielson, 2017, France/USA, 83 min.

Mi Iubita, Mon Amour. Noémie Merlant, 2021, France, 95 min.

Mignonnes (*Cuties*). Maïmouna Doucouré, 2020, France, 96 min.

Mysterious Skin. Gregg Araki, 2004, USA, 107 min.

Naissance des pieuvres (*Water Lilies*). Céline Sciamma, 2007, France, 85 min.

Les Olympiades (*Paris, 13th District*). Jacques Audiard, 2021, France, 105 min.

Pauline. Céline Sciamma, France, 8 min.

Petite Fille (*Little Girl*). Sébastien Lifschitz, France/Denmark, 90 min.

Petite Maman. Céline Sciamma, 2020, France, 72 min.

Portrait de la jeune fille en feu (*Portrait of a Lady on Fire*). Céline Sciamma, 2019, France, 122 min.

Quand on a 17 ans (*Being 17*). André Téchiné, 2016, France, 116 min.

Les 400 Coups (*The 400 Blows*). François Truffaut, 1959, France, 99 min.

Retour à Reims (Fragments)/Returning to Reims (Fragments). Jean-Gabriel Périot, 2021, France, 83 min.

La Table tournante (*Turning Table*). Jacques Demy and Paul Grimault, 1988, France, 80 min.

They. Anahita Ghazvinizadeh, 2017, USA, 80 min.

Tomboy. Céline Sciamma, 2011, France, 82 min.

Trois Places pour le 26 (*Three Seats for the 26th*). Jacques Demy, 1988, France, 106 min.

L'une chante, l'autre pas (*One Sings, The Other Doesn't*). Agnès Varda, 1977, France, 120 min.

Yamakasi – Les Samouraïs des temps modernes. Ariel Zeitoun and Julien Seri, 2001, France, 90 min.
Zéro de conduite (*Zero for Conduct*). Jean Vigo, 1933, France, 44 min.

Index